A DISCOVERY GUIDE

DINOSAURS

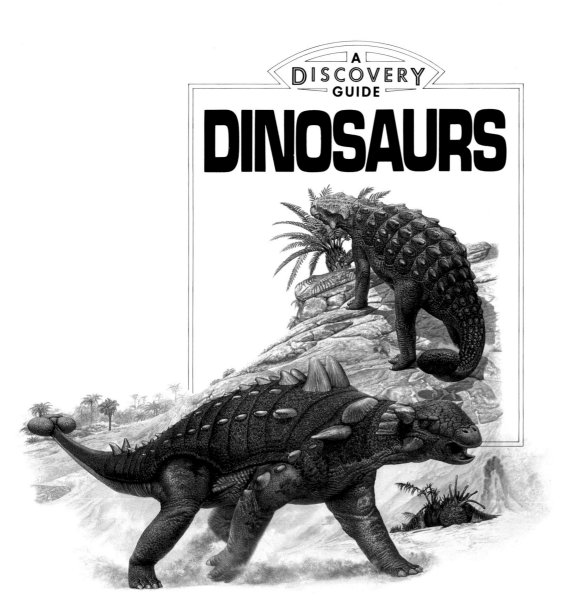

A DISCOVERY GUIDE

DINOSAURS

DR · DAVID · NORMAN

a Salamander book

Published by Salamander Books Limited

LONDON • NEW YORK

A SALAMANDER BOOK

Published by Salamander Books Ltd.,
52 Bedford Row,
London WC1R 4LR,
United Kingdom.

© Salamander Books 1989

ISBN 0 86101 448 0

Distributed in the United Kingdom by
Hodder & Stoughton Services,
PO Box 6, Mill Road,
Dunton Green, Sevenoaks,
Kent TN13 2XX.

CREDITS

Editor: Gillian Haslam
Editorial Assistant: Roseanne Eckart
Designer: SallyAnn Jackson
Colour dinosaur artwork: John Sibbick
©Salamander Books Ltd
Skeletal drawings:
Denise Blagden and David Nicholls
©Salamander Books Ltd
Typesetting: H&P Graphics Ltd
Colour separation:
by Contemporary Lithoplates Ltd
Printed in Belgium by
Proost International Book Production

THE AUTHOR

David Norman is a palaeontologist specialising in research on dinosaurs. He is head of Palaeontology at the Nature Conservancy Council of Great Britain and is responsible for the preservation of Britain's most scientifically important palaeontological sites. In addition, Dr Norman carries out scientific work as a research fellow of the University Museum, Oxford. Dr Norman has made research and collecting trips to many countries, including China, Romania, Australia, USA, Canada and western Europe. He has written several books and numerous scientific articles on dinosaurs and has appeared on radio and television.

THE ARTIST

John Sibbick studied graphic design and illustration at Guildford Art School, Surrey. He has always been interested in dinosaurs and over the last 10 years has worked on a number of books. Apart from his publishing commissions, he also works regularly for galleries and museums.

CONTENTS

INTRODUCTION	6
COELUROSAURS	12
ORNITHOMIMOSAURS & OVIRAPTOROSAURS	14
MISCELLANEOUS THEROPODS	16
SAURORNITHOIDIDS	18
DROMAEOSAURS	20
CARNOSAURS	22
TYRANNOSAURIDS	24
PROSAUROPODS	26
DIPLODOCIDS	28
CAMARASAURS & BRACHIOSAURS	30
MISCELLANEOUS SAUROPODS	32
FABROSAURS, SCUTELLOSAURUS & HETERODONTOSAURS	34
HYPSILOPHODONTIDS	36
IGUANODONTS	38
HADROSAURIDS I	40
HADROSAURIDS II	42
PSITTACOSAURS & PROTOCERATOPIDS	44
CERATOPIDS I	46
CERATOPIDS II	48
PACHYCEPHALOSAURS	50
STEGOSAURS	52
SCELIDOSAURUS	54
NODOSAURIDS	56
ANKYLOSAURIDS	58
THE EXTINCTION OF DINOSAURS	60
GEOGRAPHY OF DINOSAUR FINDS	61
GLOSSARY	62
INDEX	64

INTRODUCTION

Before launching into the main body of this book, which is devoted to describing and illustrating many of the main types of dinosaurs, we should pause for a short while to consider a few rather important questions not only about dinosaurs generally, but how they came to be and how they fit, as a group, into the larger history of the Earth.

Dinosaurs rediscovered

The last dinosaurs inhabited this Earth about 64 million years ago, that is to say at least 63.5 million years before man-like creatures appeared. Very fortunately for us, geological processes on Earth caused the burial in mud of the bodies or scattered bones of just a few of these former inhabitants, and their eventual conversion into fossils. As fossils, these precious reminders of the past could survive for tens of millions of years before being accidentally discovered, or deliberately dug up, and examined by people with interested and inquiring minds.

It would seem that dinosaur remains have been dug up in the ancient past on many occasions. Professor Dong Zhi Ming, an expert in dinosaur studies at the Institute of Vertebrate Palaeontology and Palaeoanthropology (Beijing, China) has reported that dinosaur remains, and more especially dinosaur teeth (Chinese 'Dragons' teeth'), have been dug up since the 16th century BC because they were considered to be of great medicinal value. There are even records of dragon bones having been dug up in China from the 3rd century AD, in areas of China that are now known, from modern research, to have dinosaur remains.

However, it is not to the Chinese that we turn to get our first scientific knowledge of dinosaurs, but to Britain — and considerably more recently. The first time that the word 'Dinosaur' was used was at a meeting of the British Association for the Advancement of Science at Plymouth, Devonshire in 1841. The name was coined by the anatomist Professor Richard Owen, who had been asked to present a review of all the fossil reptiles that had been discovered up to that date.

During the preparation of his review, Owen recognised that some fossil reptiles, notably *Megalosaurus* (described in 1824 by Dean William Buckland), *Iguanodon* (described by Gideon Mantell in 1825) and *Hylaeosaurus* (again described by Gideon Mantell, but this time in 1833), were all very

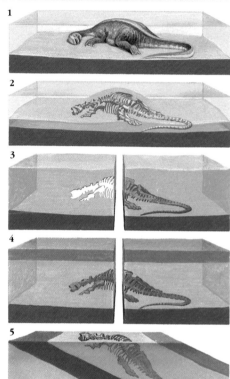

Left: *Fossilisation*
An essential requirement for the formation of a fossil is that after the organism dies (1) and the soft tissues rot away leaving (in this example) the bony skeleton, it should be rapidly buried by sediment (2). This normally occurs in rivers, lakes or the sea into which the carcasses of land-living animals may be washed. Two processes may then occur (3). The organic material in the body decays and may be replaced by minerals from water percolating through the sedimentary rocks: permineralisation (left). The bony structure may even be replaced entirely by minerals: petrification. Alternatively the bones may dissolve leaving a hollow mould (right) which may be filled by minerals which form a solid replica of the bone: a natural cast (4 right). Land movements and erosion then lead to the exposure of the fossil.

Right: *The Geological Timescale*
Each twist of this spiral covers 570 million years of the Earth's history. The Earth was formed from a cloud of dust about 4,500 million years ago (mya). As it cooled a crust formed, and gas and water vapour formed an atmosphere of dense cloud and poisonous gas. By 3,000 mya the crust and atmosphere were stable enough for the first living organisms to appear — simple, single-celled bacteria. The next 2,400 million years were dominated by simple forms of life, mainly bacteria living on simple chemicals, and others ('blue-greens') using sunlight to make oxygen. The blue-green algae formed stromalites (huge reef-like structures) in the oceans. Complex organisms appeared 600 mya, after which evolution proceeded rapidly. The age of dinosaurs (225-64 mya) is visible on the top layer.

Below: *Sedimentation*
Weathering of upland areas is responsible for the formation of sedimentary rocks. Wind, water, rain and ice erode exposed rock; the silt is carried to deltas, lagoons or lakes to be deposited in layers. Land-living animals are most likely to be fossilised in such areas.

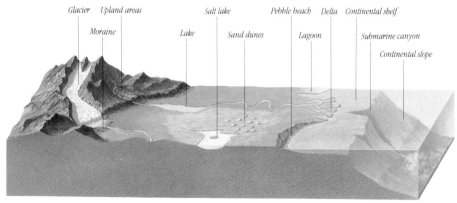

Glacier Upland areas Salt lake Pebble beach Delta Continental shelf
Moraine Lake Sand dunes Lagoon Submarine canyon
Continental slope

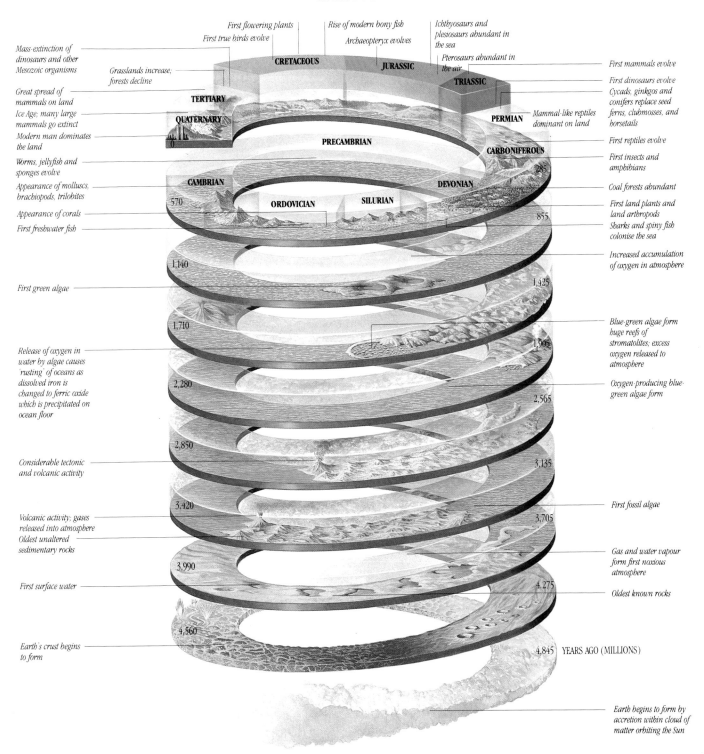

First flowering plants

First true birds evolve

Rise of modern bony fish

Archaeopteryx evolves

Ichthyosaurs and plesiosaurs abundant in the sea

Pterosaurs abundant in the air

Mass-extinction of dinosaurs and other Mesozoic organisms

Grasslands increase; forests decline

CRETACEOUS

JURASSIC

TRIASSIC

First mammals evolve

First dinosaurs evolve

Great spread of mammals on land

TERTIARY

Cycads, ginkgos and conifers replace seed ferns, clubmosses, and horsetails

Ice Age; many large mammals go extinct

QUATERNARY

PERMIAN

Mammal-like reptiles dominant on land

Modern man dominates the land

0

PRECAMBRIAN

CARBONIFEROUS

First reptiles evolve

Worms, jellyfish and sponges evolve

285

First insects and amphibians

Appearance of molluscs, brachiopods, trilobites

CAMBRIAN

DEVONIAN

Coal forests abundant

570

Appearance of corals

ORDOVICIAN

SILURIAN

First land plants and land arthropods

First freshwater fish

855

Sharks and spiny fish colonise the sea

1,140

Increased accumulation of oxygen in atmosphere

First green algae

1,425

1,710

Blue-green algae form huge reefs of stromatolites; excess oxygen released to atmosphere

1,905

Release of oxygen in water by algae causes 'rusting' of oceans as dissolved iron is changed to ferric oxide which is precipitated on ocean floor

2,280

Oxygen-producing blue-green algae form

2,565

2,850

Considerable tectonic and volcanic activity

3,135

3,420

First fossil algae

Volcanic activity; gases released into atmosphere

3,705

Oldest unaltered sedimentary rocks

3,990

Gas and water vapour form first noxious atmosphere

First surface water

4,275

Oldest known rocks

4,560

Earth's crust begins to form

4,845   YEARS AGO (MILLIONS)

Earth begins to form by accretion within cloud of matter orbiting the Sun

7

different from other fossil reptiles and from living ones as well. These reptiles tended to be large (up to elephant sized — or so he thought) and, unlike all other reptiles, walked on long, pillar-like legs which were tucked under the body, rather than being splayed out to the sides (as is normally the case in reptiles). Indeed Owen saw many similarities between these peculiar reptiles and modern large mammals such as rhinoceroses, hippopotamuses and elephants and imagined that these strange reptiles represented the peak of reptile evolution because they paralleled the mammals of today. To recognise this difference Owen used the name 'Dinosaur', derived from two Greek words: *deinos* (meaning 'fearfully great') and *sauros* (meaning 'crawling animal' or reptile).

Owen was very far sighted to have recognised the importance of these reptiles, especially as they were based on the few fragmentary bits and pieces known at the time. As it turned out, his views about the appearance of these animals were far from correct, but that only became apparent after better and more complete specimens of dinosaurs were discovered nearly forty years later. The important fact is that Owen recognised the importance of the group, gave them a name and fired off a whole new area of research which has continued through to the present day.

How are dinosaurs recognised?

Dinosaurs, as Owen recognised, are not just any group of fossil animals. First and foremost they are reptiles, which means that like living reptiles they have scaly skin and lay shelled eggs (both skin impressions and fossil eggs of dinosaurs have been found, so we can actually confirm this). Secondly, they lived during the Mesozoic Era (more precisely between about 215 and 64 million years ago — from the end of the Triassic Period until the end of the Cretaceous Period). Thirdly, all dinosaurs were land-livers, none habitually swam (even though some may have taken to the water occasionally — this means that the giant sea reptiles of the Mesozoic were *not* dinosaurs) or flew (so the flying reptiles or pterosaurs of the Mesozoic were *not* dinosaurs).

Most importantly, as Owen pointed out long ago, they were able to walk and run more efficiently than any living reptile because their legs were tucked in beneath their bodies, rather than being held out from their sides. This has left tell-tale changes in

Above: *Richard Owen (1804-1892) who first coined the term 'Dinosauria'. He became the first superintendent of the British Museum (Natural History).*

Below: *Hip Structure The top hip is the pelvis of an early ornithischian dinosaur. Note the position of the pubis (in red). The bottom is a typical saurischian pelvis.*

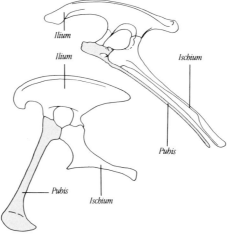

Ilium
Ilium
Ischium
Pubis
Pubis
Ischium

the shape of the bones of the hip, knee and ankle. The fossilised remains of these bones and joints clearly distinguish dinosaur remains from those of other archosaurs.

The nearest living relatives of dinosaurs are birds, and it should be noted that some dinosaurs, especially the small carnivorous ones (see pages 12-20 in particular) do show some similarities to flightless birds — especially the large ground dwelling ones such as ostriches, emus and rheas.

Dinosaur classification

There are now many hundreds of species of dinosaur known. Since the last half of the nineteenth century, these have been recognised as being split into two quite distinct groups known as **Ornithischians** and **Saurischians**.

These two names actually refer to the arrangement of the three hip bones (the ilium, pubis and ischium) of dinosaurs (see illustration below).

Saurischian dinosaurs

The name means literally 'reptile hipped' and refers to the fact that the bones of the pelvis are arranged similarly to the way that they are in most reptiles. The hip comprises three bones, which radiate out in different directions from the centre where they form the hip socket. This arrangement provides an area for the attachment of large leg-moving muscles. The ilium contacts the backbone, forming a very solid attachment.

This group of dinosaurs includes all the meat-eating dinosaurs commonly known as **theropods**, (pages 12-25) and a variety of large and medium-sized plant eaters known as **sauropodomorphs**, ranging from the relatively small **prosauropods** (pages 26-27), to the gigantic **sauropods** (pages 28-33).

Ornithischian dinosaurs

This name means 'bird hipped' because the arrangement of the hip bones is similar to that seen in living birds. Comparing the hip bones of *Compsognathus* (a typical theropod saurischian) with *Heterodontosaurus* (a small ornithischian) in the illustration it can be seen that while the upper (ilium) and rear (ischium) hip bones are more or less the same in both species, the pubis is very different. Most of the bone lies parallel to the ischium in the ornithischian.

Other differences include the possession of a small horny beak at the tip of the jaw in ornithischians (examine the illustrations carefully), and the occurrence of bony rods (ossified tendons) along the sides of the backbone, which are not found in saurischians at all.

Ornithischians are all herbivorous (hence the plant-nipping beak) and include quite varied groups of dinosaurs compared with saurischians. They include **ornithopods** (pages 34-43), **ceratopians** (pages 44-49), **pachycephalosaurs** (pages 50-51), **stegosaurs** (pages 52-53) and **ankylosaurs** (pages 56-59).

Right: *Between 1852 and 1854 Richard Owen and the sculptor Waterhouse Hawkins produced several life-sized models of dinosaurs and other prehistoric animals for the grounds of the Crystal Palace exhibition centre at Sydenham, London. Just before they completed their task, Owen and Hawkins organised a dinner party for 20 people inside the incomplete body of an Iguanodon. As seen in the engraving of the occasion, the guests were rather cramped! The models attracted huge publicity and are still standing today. Even though we now know them to be inaccurate, they still create a strong impression on the viewer.*

Dinosaur discoveries

The first scientific descriptions of dinosaurs began to appear in the 1820s, through the work of Dean William Buckland (Professor of Geology at the University of Oxford) and Gideon Algernon Mantell (medical doctor and amateur geologist based in Sussex) and their description of incomplete remains of *Megalosaurus* (a large theropod), *Iguanodon* (an ornithopod) and *Hylaeosaurus* (an ankylosaur). Although these were eventually named as dinosaurs by Owen in 1841, much confusion remained over their appearance because they were only known from scrappy remains – insufficient for an accurate reconstruction. Owen reasoned that they may have looked like giant, scaly rhinoceroses or elephants and had models made of these in 1853. However it was not until the late 1870s, half a century after the first descriptions were published, that good skeletons were found almost simultaneously in North America and in Europe.

In 1877 fossils were discovered in Colorado by two amateur collectors. These fossils were sent to two palaeontologists: Edward Drinker Cope and Othniel Charles Marsh. These two men of science fought a life-long battle to describe the first and best of any new dinosaur discoveries, but the products of their feud were some magnificent dinosaur collections and over 130 new dinosaur names! Teams of collectors travelled far and wide across the American West (mainly in the states of Colorado, Wyoming and Montana, but spreading as far afield as New Jersey and New Mexico). Since the time of Cope and Marsh, collecting has continued in many parts of North America, either expanding on the areas covered by Marsh and Cope, or by the discovery of new areas.

The initiatives of Cope and Marsh were rapidly followed around the turn of the century by collecting parties from the American Museum of Natural History in New York, going out to Wyoming. Eventually, in the summer of 1898, just north of Como Bluff in Wyoming, a new locality was discovered which proved to be very rich in fossils. The place which the collectors stumbled across was called Bone Cabin Quarry – a hillside literally strewn with fragments of dinosaur bones. So abundant were the bones in this area that a shepherd had used them to build himself a small shelter – the 'Bone Cabin' after which the quarry was named. The American Museum worked the area for many years and collected a vast quantity of dinosaur bones, many of which are now on display in the museum.

Another great American museum was also very actively collecting fossils at this time, the Carnegie Museum of Pittsburgh which had been founded by Andrew Carnegie (the American industrialist and philanthropist). In 1908/1909 Earl Douglass, hired by the Museum as a collector and preparator of fossils, discovered dinosaur remains near the town of Vernal in Utah, and very shortly found a complete skeleton of the giant sauropod *Apatosaurus* (page 28). A large quarrying operation was set up to recover this skeleton and the many other dinosaur remains that began to appear in the area. Indeed this area proved to be so rich for dinosaurs, with good skeletons of *Diplodocus, Camarasaurus, Stegosaurus* and *Allosaurus* being recovered, that in 1915 the area became protected by government legislation and was named 'Dinosaur National Monument'. Today Dinosaur National Monument is a working museum and visitor centre, with the highly fossiliferous bed of rock exposed for visitors to view while skilled workers slowly prepare new fossils.

At the time that Earl Douglass was stumbling upon the remains of dinosaurs in Utah, teams of fossil collectors were very active in Africa. In particular, a team of workers from Germany (the Berlin Museum of Natural History) were excavating fossils from Tendaguru in what was then German East Africa (now Tanzania). With the help of teams of native Africans, some spectacular finds were made, the most notable being the immense skeleton of *Brachiosaurus*, the tallest mounted dinosaur in the world (page 30).

Indeed the early years of this century were a time of very many dinosaur discoveries. The first two decades saw the opening up of areas of western Canada (Alberta), particularly in the area of the Red Deer River, and the discovery of large numbers of dinosaurs, some of which went to New York, and others to the large Canadian museums in Ottawa and Toronto.

The new new and really exciting initiative was again taken by the American Museum of Natural History in New York, during the 1920s. An expedition was arranged by Walter Granger of the museum staff, along with Roy Chapman Andrews and Henry Fairfield Osborn with the intention of going to Mongolia and Northern China in search of Man's ancestors. To their great surprise they found a remarkable cache of dinosaurs. Most of these dinosaurs were completely new to science (*Protoceratops, Velociraptor, Saurornithoides, Oviraptor, Pinacosaurus* and *Psittacosaurus*). But in addition, for the first time they also found dinosaur eggs and nests of *Protoceratops*. Since that time there have been various follow-up expeditions to the same areas by Swedish, Polish, Russian and Chinese teams in association with Mongolian scientists, all of which have produced interesting and important discoveries.

In recent years dinosaur collecting expeditions have gone to other parts of Africa (Mali, Niger, Morocco and Kenya), as well as to South America (particularly Argentina, which has a very rich fossil record of dinosaurs), Australia (which is just beginning to show evidence of a distinct dinosaur fauna) and India (which is well known for its Jurassic and late Cretaceous dinosaurs).

All continents have now yielded dinosaurs, with a new dinosaur having recently been collected from Antarctica. It appears to be a hypsilophodontid and was discovered in late Cretaceous rocks.

Rocks and time

It is estimated that the Earth is 4600 million years old, and the oldest known rocks are 3500 million years old. Life, in its very simplest form appeared about 3000 million years ago, but it is not until the relatively recent (less than 600 million years ago) that more complex forms of life are known.

Dinosaurs first appeared on Earth as recognisable fossils about 215 million years ago, in the late part of the Triassic Period and persisted through the following Jurassic Period and into the Cretaceous Period until their apparent sudden extinction right at the end of the Cretaceous Period 64 million years ago. As a group, therefore, dinosaurs last some 150 million years. That is not to say that all dinosaurs lived that long, merely that the groups lived during that time. Many groups of dinosaur lived and became extinct during this immense period of time.

Plate tectonics

During the 150 million years of Earth history when dinosaurs lived, the surface of the Earth was surprising active. It is now a well known fact that the outer layer or crust of our planet is divided into a series of gigantic plates (*tectonic* plates) which operate a little bit like enormous conveyor belts: they are being constantly pushed apart along mountain-like *ridges*, and are disappearing along deep ocean *trenches*. These plates move very slowly (a matter of a few centimetres a year in general), but as they move they carry along the continents. Incredible though it seems, the continents upon which we live are quite light compared with the earth's crust and so are able to literally float upon these moving plates.

During the reign of the dinosaurs, the continents started quite close together at first (late Triassic times) but gradually separated. For example, Europe and North America drifted apart to the point where western North America came close to eastern Asia. The maps on this page show the dramatic movement of the continents throughout the Mesozoic Era. These movements affected the distribution of dinosaurs on worldwide basis and influenced their evolutionary history. The maps on the following pages show the various positions of the continents during the Triassic, Jurassic and Cretaceous Periods and the locations of dinosaur remains.

Dinosaur origins

The origin of dinosaurs is a subject still argued about today. The first appearance of dinosaurs may have been linked to a number of factors, such as their development of very efficient ways of walking and running, a

change to the hotter, arid conditions that suit reptiles very well, or alternatively it could be down to pure luck giving dinosaurs the chance to develop.

The most popular of the current theories concerning dinosaur origins and success depends upon an understanding of the way in which reptiles move. As Owen pointed out all those years ago, dinosaurs differ from normal reptiles because they have legs which are arranged more like those of mammals and birds: they are long, and are tucked beneath the body so that movement is much more efficient than in typical modern reptiles (lizards, crocodiles, tortoises) in which the legs tend to be short and stick outward from

Left: *Palaeogeographic Maps*

Study of continental drift has made possible the production of a series of maps showing continental positions as they were in the Mesozoic Era. In the Triassic Period (1) all the continents were joined together to form the supercontinent of Pangaea. This began to split in the Jurassic Period (2); a narrow Atlantic Ocean formed and sea separated Asia and Europe. By the early Cretaceous period (3), the continents were further removed, and shallow seas divided the southern continents. By late Cretaceous times (4), South America and Africa were separating, India was rafting away across the Indian Ocean and North America and Europe were moving apart. Seas divided Europe and Asia, and western from eastern North America, resulting in strangely isolated fauna.

the sides of the body, so that the belly is almost dragged along the ground when they walk or run.

This observation has been turned into a theory to explain the success of dinosaurs in the Triassic. It is claimed that the dinosaurs were the first of a number of groups of animals living at about this time to fully develop this leg position (with all the advantages that it would give them for running fast, and for supporting heavier or larger bodies). Because they were 'first past the post' – to use a running analogy – early dinosaurs were able to run faster to catch their prey, and therefore out-competed other land carnivores (such as mammal-like reptiles) causing their extinction, and the extinction of their prey animals, leading to the rise to dominance of the dinosaurs as a group. Although this might seem at first sight

to be a reasonable theory, it flies in the face of our knowledge of normal predator-prey interactions.

An alternative theory for dinosaur success is that the key was in climatic changes at the time. It is thought that conditions in the late Triassic were becoming increasingly hot and dry, which would very much favour reptiles which rely on obtaining heat from the environment to keep their bodies warm, rather than the mammals (or mammal-like reptiles) which would have used internal body heat production. It is certainly true that mammals today find hot dry desert conditions most stressful because of the high temperatures, lack of water (they need to sweat to keep themselves cool) and lack of food; whereas reptiles can cope more easily with these conditions.

The problem with this theory is proving

that the environmental conditions were precisely as has been proposed: hot and dry. Not everyone agrees!

A third alternative is that dinosaurs had a lucky escape! Detailed analysis of fossil finds from rocks from the Triassic period reveals that a major unknown event caused the extinction of many land animals in the late Triassic. Dinosaurs were not affected and simply evolved into the space left by the departed animals in an opportunistic way. To be able to prove this theory it is essential to be able to make an accurate estimate of the numbers of animals living through the late Triassic in order to see whether there is a clear extinction of animals before the dinosaurs appear. However, this is obviously very difficult to do because our knowledge of the precise numbers of creatures living before the age of dinosaurs is extremely limited.

COELUROSAURS

Pronunciation:	See-lure-oh-sores
Includes:	Ornitholestes, Compsognathus, Coelophysis
Period:	Late Triassic to mid-Cretaceous
	(215-100 mya)
Location:	Western North America, western Europe,
	eastern and southern Africa, Australia, China

Coelurosaurs are a rather vague group of dinosaurs since they do not all belong to the same related group or family. They are instead an assortment of small carnivorous dinosaurs. Drawing a comparison with animals living today, it is rather like calling 'small carnivores' a natural group which might include weasels, badgers, lions, cheetahs and dogs. Clearly these are all mammals and eat meat, but weasels are not particularly close relatives of lions, even though lions and cheetahs are fairly closely related.

Coelurosaurs are generally small, meat-eating, theropod dinosaurs. The name coelurosaur literally means 'hollow tailed', and derives from the fact that the first remains ever described were tail bones, the broken ends revealing that they were light and spongy.

All coelurosaurs are small (under 3 metres (10 ft) long) when compared with the great majority of theropod dinosaurs (see pages 16-17). They all tend to have rather small heads, with slender jaws armed with narrow, curved and serrated teeth. The vertebral column is long and flexible, indicating animals which are lithe and swiftly moving. The legs are long and slender and designed in such a way that they could run very fast on bird-like three toed feet. The arms tend to be long and end in sharply clawed fingers. The hand is typically three fingered as it is in

Below: Coelophysis
This slim dinosaur could have run on its hind legs or walked on all-fours. The three strong fingers on each hand were used for attacking prey. This is one of the earliest and most primitive dinosaurs.

Below: Ornitholestes
This dinosaur was about 2 m (6.5 ft) long with strong jaws and powerful grasping hands for catching prey.

Above: Compsognathus
One of the smallest dinosaurs, **Compsognathus** *reached a total length of only 70 cm (28 in). Most of this length was made up by the long slender tail which was used as a balancing rod during running. One unusual feature of* **Compsognathus** *was the hand with its two clawed fingers.*

Ornitholestes, but the examples here show that this can vary quite a lot: *Compsognathus* has only two functional fingers (the third finger is represented by a vestigial metacarpal), while *Coelophysis* has a remnant of a fourth finger.

The long slender tail seen in all these examples is used to counterbalance the front half of the body, and may also serve as a dynamic stabiliser to assist with rapid changes of direction when these animals are chasing rapidly moving and elusive prey.

Precisely what these animals ate is uncertain in most instances although it is possible to make fairly intelligent guesses, and in rather rare instances to get some more convincing evidence. As small and agile creatures (somewhat akin to dogs and small cats living today) it is possible to imagine that these animals fed upon creatures that were smaller than themselves, such as the young of other dinosaurs, lizards, small mouse or shrew-like mammals; they may even have scavenged upon the carcasses of animals left by other more accomplished killers.

In the case of *Compsognathus* we seem to have some of the best evidence concerning diet. Professor John Ostrom (Yale University) described the partial skeleton of a small lizard (*Bavarisaurus*) within the rib cage of *Compsognathus*. This had almost certainly been eaten by *Compsognathus*. For *Coelophysis* the evidence appears to be a little more gruesome. Several skeletons,

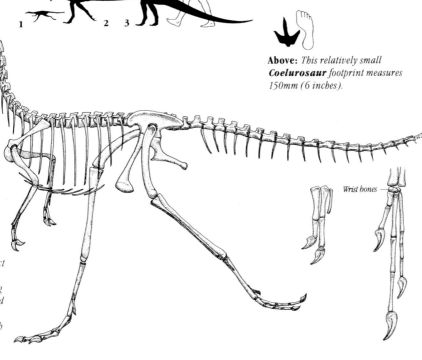

Map (left)

1	Aristosuchus	7	Kakuru
2	Coelophysis	8	Longosaurus
3	Coelurus	9	Lukousaurus
4	Compsognathus	10	Ornitholestes
5	Elaphrosaurus	11	Procompsognathus
6	Halticosaurus	12	Saltopus
		13	Syntarsus

found in a large graveyard of *Coelophysis* at Ghost Ranch in Texas, show the remains of small *Coelophysis* skeletons inside. This does not appear to be a case of pregnant female *Coelophysis* being preserved, but more likely of cannibalism. Similar occurrences are known to happen today with lions killing lion cubs, so we should not ascribe this nasty habit just to dinosaurs!

Ornitholestes is the least well known of the dinosaurs illustrated below. One incomplete skeleton, discovered at Bone Cabin Quarry in Wyoming in 1900, has been described to date and this shows an animal with normal coelurosaur proportions, and a quite large, strong head. Compared to *Coelophysis* and *Compsognathus*, the hands are also large and powerful with long clawed fingers providing an effective gripping mechanism. This combination suggests that *Ornitholestes* may have preferred to capture larger and stronger prey.

Left: *Comparative sizes*
1 *Compsognathus: 70cm-1.4m (28in-4.6ft)*
2 *Ornitholestes: 2m (6.5ft)*
3 *Coelophysis: 3m (10ft)*

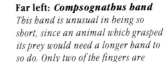

Above: *This relatively small* **Coelurosaur** *footprint measures 150mm (6 inches).*

**Right:
*Compsognathus***
This skeleton is lightly built as these animals were fairly small. The neck is long and flexible and joins onto a rather compact body. This creature is bipedal with strong slender back legs and reduced, but still useful, front legs with strong claws.

Wrist bones

Far left: *Compsognathus hand*
This hand is unusual in being so short, since an animal which grasped its prey would need a longer hand to so do. Only two of the fingers are clawed and the third is very small.

Left: *Ornitholestes hand*
This hand has two especially long fingers and a short first finger. The short finger may have turned inwards (like a thumb) to help hold onto prey.

ORNITHOMIMOSAURS & OVIRAPTOROSAURS

Pronunciation:	Or-nith-oh-mi-moh-sores
	Ove-ih-rap-tor-oh-sores
Includes:	Struthiomimus, Dromiceiomimus,
	Gallimimus, Garudimimus, Elaphrosaurus,
	Oviraptor
Period:	Late Cretaceous
	(110-64 mya)
Location:	Western North America, China

Below: *Struthiomimus*
The proportions of the body of this dinosaur and many of its features are similar to today's ostrich.

While both of these groups of dinosaurs are included with the other more typical theropods (as on page 16) they are very different in one very important respect: they have no teeth. Their jaws are in fact lined with a broad, but sharp, horny beak (similar to that of a turtle or tortoise). They do not even have the sharp hooked beak similar to a bird of prey that would perhaps be expected. This is very unusual among car-nivorous dinosaurs which almost invariably have their jaws lined with formidable rows of sharp, curved, serrated teeth. In all other respects these types of dinosaur are like 'coelurosaurs' such as those described on pages 12 and 13; they have long necks, small heads, long grasping arms, very long legs for running at great speeds and a long balancing tail.

Ornithomimosaurs (the name means 'bird mimic reptiles') are often referred to as 'ostrich dinosaurs' because they do seem to bear an uncanny resemblance to living ostriches—without the feathers of course! These dino-saurs have been collected from rocks of the late Cretaceous period (80-64 million years ago) in North America and Asia.

Struthiomimus (ostrich mimic) was found in the early years of this century in North America firstly as a few isolated bones, but just a few years later in the form of a nearly complete skeleton, which can now be seen in the American Museum of Natural History (New York).

The habits of *Struthiomimus* can be guessed at with a fair amount of precision from com-parisons made between animals such as this and similar living types: the large flightless run-ning birds of the southern con-tinents (ostrich, emu, and casso-wary). The long hind legs were clearly for fast running, and added to this, the tail provided a counterbalance for the front half of the body, so that it was well balanced at the hips, and also allowed space to attach the large and powerful leg muscles. The rather low, slender skull was pro-bably quite flexible and allowed these creatures to eat a whole

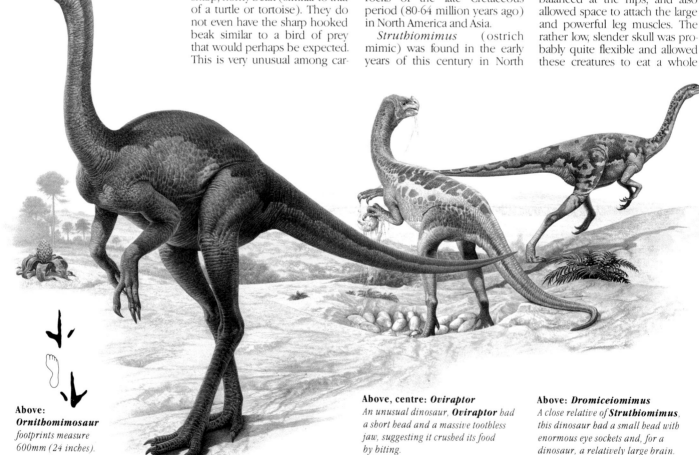

Above:
Ornithomimosaur
footprints measure 600mm (24 inches).

Above, centre: *Oviraptor*
*An unusual dinosaur, **Oviraptor** had a short head and a massive toothless jaw, suggesting it crushed its food by biting.*

Above: *Dromiceiomimus*
*A close relative of **Struthiomimus**, this dinosaur had a small head with enormous eye sockets and, for a dinosaur, a relatively large brain.*

range of food ranging from fruits and berries to a variety of insects, small lizards and mammals. The eyes of *Struthiomimus* were very large and their vision would undoubtedly have been acute for following small darting creatures. One major advantage which ornithomimosaurs would have gained over ground birds of today was the fact that they had arms with powerful three-clawed hands, rather than stubby little wings; these would have been very useful for catching prey, or picking other items of food.

Dromiceiomimus, also from North America, is in most res-

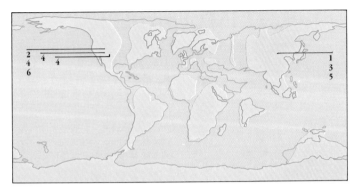

Map (left)
1 *Deinocheirus*
2 *Dromiceiomimus*
3 *Gallimimus*
4 *Ornithomimus*
5 *Oviraptor*
6 *Struthiomimus*

pects very similar to *Struthiomimus*, but differs in that it has a shorter back, a rather more slender forearm and hand and slightly different shaped hips.

There are several types of ornithomimosaur, including forms such as *Gallimimus* ('chicken-like reptile') and *Garudimimus* ('mythical bird imitator') from Asia and *Elaphrosaurus* ('light reptile') from Africa.

Oviraptorosaurs (the name means literally 'egg stealing reptiles') are extraordinary, but unfortunately poorly known creatures. It is not at all clear whether they are close relatives of the ornithomimosaurs; they are really included here because, as in the former group, these dinosaurs lack teeth.

The first remains of *Oviraptor* were discovered in Mongolia in the 1920's by an American expedition. The remains were actually

found atop a nest of *Protoceratops* eggs — almost as if caught in the act of stealing them! The skull is rather short, and has many large openings including those for the eyes. It certainly seems possible that this type of creature preyed upon nests of dinosaur eggs; the short powerful jaws would be ideal for cracking open the thick shells, but they may have been general scavengers as well.

A recent joint China-Canada expedition to Inner Mongolia has reported the discovery of more material of *Oviraptor*, which may help us to learn more about this extraordinary animal.

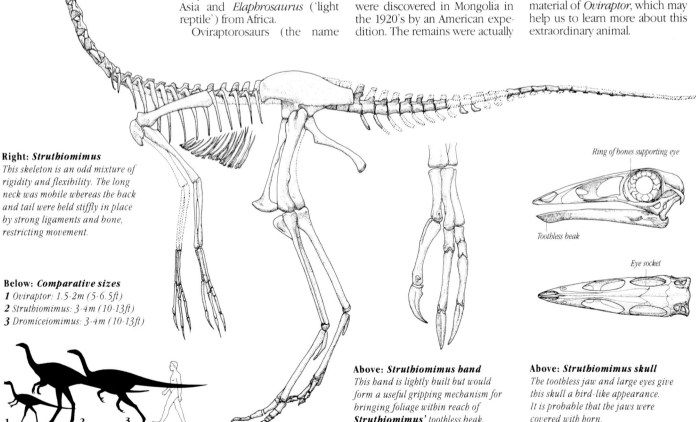

Right: *Struthiomimus*
This skeleton is an odd mixture of rigidity and flexibility. The long neck was mobile whereas the back and tail were held stiffly in place by strong ligaments and bone, restricting movement.

Below: *Comparative sizes*
1 Oviraptor: 1.5-2m (5-6.5ft)
2 Struthiomimus: 3-4m (10-13ft)
3 Dromiceiomimus: 3-4m (10-13ft)

Ring of bones supporting eye

Toothless beak

Eye socket

Above: *Struthiomimus hand*
*This hand is lightly built but would form a useful gripping mechanism for bringing foliage within reach of **Struthiomimus'** toothless beak.*

Above: *Struthiomimus skull*
The toothless jaw and large eyes give this skull a bird-like appearance. It is probable that the jaws were covered with horn.

MISCELLANEOUS THEROPODS

Pronunciation:	Ther-oh-pods
Includes:	Segisaurus, Avimimus, Segnosaurus, Erlikosaurus
Period:	Early Jurassic (Segisaurus) (190-180 mya) Late Cretaceous (80-64 mya)
Location:	Western North America, South America, China

During the past decade a large number of dinosaurs have been described particularly through new expeditions in China, Mongolia and, to a lesser extent, North America. While several of the new finds have been of well preserved dinosaurs, an even larger number of finds have been made which are of fossil animals and are far from complete. The fact that material is incomplete means that it is much more difficult to compare it to what is already known. In such circumstances, it is sometimes safer for the scientist to give the material a new name for simple identification purposes. Unfortunately this also leads to the appearance of many names for animals which, when

Left: Segnosaur
*This is a hypothetical animal. At present we know the structure of the **Erlikosaurus'** skull plus part of the jaw, legs, pelvis, hands and feet of **Segnosaurus**. These have been joined together to give an impression of a **Segnosaur's** appearance.*

Right: Avimimus
This dinosaur is shown with a feather-like covering on its body. Some bones of the body, particularly the arms, show traces equivalent to the feather attachment areas on birds, suggesting that some theropods were feathered.

Left: Segisaurus
This dinosaur was small and lightly constructed and was presumably an agile runner. It probably fed on small vertebrates or insects, but as the teeth were not preserved we cannot be sure of its diet.

Above: *A theropod footprint measuring 250mm (10 inches).*

Right: Comparative sizes
1 Segisaurus: 1m (3.3ft)
2 Avimimus: 1.5m (5ft)
3 Segnosaur: 4.6m (15ft)

they are further studied, or when new material is discovered, may turn out to belong to a previously known type. This 'Miscellaneous Theropods' page is simply a way of making the point that our scientific knowledge of many dinosaurs is far from complete and in some cases positively confusing. Below are some species of theropod dinosaur which have caused many problems.

Segisaurus consists of the headless, partial skeleton of a dinosaur found in Arizona. It comes from rocks which are from the early Jurassic Period and is a small creature 1 metre (3 ft) long. Without a head, and with many other parts of its anatomy unknown, it is impossible to be sure of its closest

relatives among the Theropoda. However it is an approximate contemporary of *Coelophysis* and may well be a small individual either of this type, or of an animal quite closely related to *Coelophysis*.

Avimimus is a bird-like dinosaur which comes from the late Cretaceous of Mongolia and was described by Dr Sergei Kurzanov of Moscow who suggested that it is a bird-like theropod and that it may even have had feathers on its arms (see colour illustration). The animal has an extraordinary mixture of dinosaur and bird characters; it has the hips, legs and feet of a theropod and yet some of its vertebrae and parts of its hands are very like those of birds. The tip of the jaw is

also very bird-like because it is toothless, and the braincase appears to resemble (of all things) that of a small sauropod dinosaur! This extraordinary dinosaur was not, unfortunately, found as a complete fossil skeleton, so until more material turns up we remain mystified by it.

Segnosaurus is a late cretaceous form that was first reported by Drs Altangerel Perle and Rinchen Barsbold of Ulan Bator (Mongolia) in 1979. The remains of this animal are frustratingly incomplete. One of its most notable characteristics is the fact that the pelvis is very similar to that of birds (the pubis pointing backwards alongside the ischium, instead of diagonally away from the ischium). The

front of the jaws is unusual because it appears to lack teeth, even though there are small sharp teeth further back in the mouth.

More material of an apparently close relative of *Segnosaurus* named *Erlikosaurus* includes a skull, which shows very clearly the toothless front part of the jaw; this was probably covered by a horny beak.

Quite how forms like *Segnosaurus* and *Erlikosaurus* are related to other dinosaurs is uncertain; they may not even be theropods. One recent suggestion is that they are late surviving relatives of the prosauropods (page 26) which are only otherwise known of in the late Triassic and early Jurassic.

Below: *Segisaurus skeleton*
*The skeleton of **Segisaurus** is rather badly preserved and unfortunately headless. The fragmentary remains*

included back vertebrae, ribs, shoulder girdle, arms, legs and pelvis. It was evidently a small, agile theropod with short arms and powerful grasping hands. The absence of a head is frustrating since it might have revealed its diet, and relationship to other theropods.

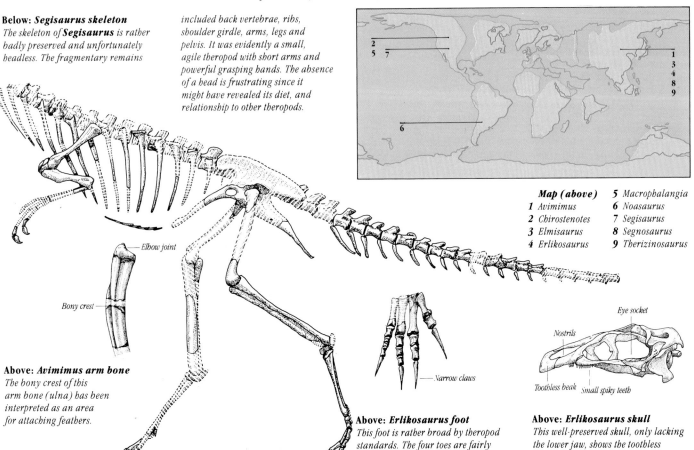

Map (above)
1 *Avimimus*	**5** *Macrophalangia*
2 *Chirostenotes*	**6** *Noasaurus*
3 *Elmisaurus*	**7** *Segisaurus*
4 *Erlikosaurus*	**8** *Segnosaurus*
	9 *Therizinosaurus*

Elbow joint

Bony crest

Above: *Avimimus arm bone*
The bony crest of this arm bone (ulna) has been interpreted as an area for attaching feathers.

Narrow claws

Above: *Erlikosaurus foot*
This foot is rather broad by theropod standards. The four toes are fairly short, ending in narrow claws.

Eye socket

Nostrils

Toothless beak   Small spiky teeth

Above: *Erlikosaurus skull*
This well-preserved skull, only lacking the lower jaw, shows the toothless beak and pointed teeth.

17

SAURORNITHOIDIDS

Pronunciation:	Sore-or-nith-oy-dids
Includes:	Saurornithoides, Stenonychosaurus
Period:	Late Cretaceous
	(85-70 mya)
Location:	Western North America, China

Below: *Dinosauroid*
Russell and Séguin's **Dinosauroid** is illustrated here with an enlarged brain, a short neck and vertical posture, eliminating the need for a tail. The legs were modified by lowering the ankle to the ground.

As was the case with the oviraptorosaurs (page 14), this group of dinosaurs first became known as a result of the enormously successful American Central Asiatic Expedition to Mongolia and China in the 1920's. The first remains came from Bain Dzak (Shabarakh Usu is the original mongolian name of the place), otherwise known to palaeontologists the world over as 'The Flaming Cliffs' after the beautiful red sandstone cliffs that surround this locality. Most of a skull was discovered and, a little way off, parts of the back, hips, legs and feet were recovered as well.

Saurornithoides mongoliensis ('bird-like reptile from Mongolia'), when first discovered, was thought to be the remains of an early toothed bird. In the rock, the fossil skull had a rather long and narrow bird-like snout, and it was known that early birds had teeth. However it was soon realised that these were the remains of a medium-sized predatory dinosaur.

In general appearance *Saurornithoides* resembles the ornithomimosaurs of page 14. However, there are one or two critical differences. The jaws are lined with large numbers of teeth, which are not particulary big, but are narrow and curved and have only one main cutting edge; this is at the rear of the tooth, where there are a series of large, jagged, serrations. Most carnivorous dinosaurs have serrations along both the front and rear edges of their teeth. Careful investigation of the feet of these dinosaurs will also reveal another crucial difference. The first toe is small and backwards curved (as in the majority of theropods), but the second is not a typical walking toe. The toe ends in a somewhat enlarged sickle-shaped claw which was probably held away from the ground to avoid becoming blunt. (A much more elaborate claw of this type is to be seen in the foot of the next group of dinosaurs, the dromaeosaurs, page 20.)

Further fragmentary discoveries of this type of dinosaur have been made in North America and Asia in more recent years and in 1974 Rinchen Barsbold, the leading dinosaur worker in Mongolia, described more material of *Saurornithoides*. This belonged to a larger animal, but was otherwise quite similar, but added a little more to our knowledge of this group. In particular it was discovered that these dinosaurs have peculiar swollen areas under the braincase and around the ear, although it is not immediately apparent what these areas were used for in the living dinosaur.

Stenonychosaurus is the North American equivalent of the Asian *Saurornithoides*. For much of this century, all that was known of this animal was based on its hands and feet (which were similar to those of *Saurornithoides*). However in 1967 a new partial skeleton was described from Alberta which forms the basis of the restoration given here.

In 1982 Dale Russell and R. Séguin of Ottawa published an interesting article in which they attempted to extend the evolution of dinosaurs through to the present day. They posed the question: Which of all the dinosaurs could have become the most intelligent and perhaps man-like given the appropriate evolutionary pressures? Their answer was the saurornithoidids. These dinosaurs seemed to them to possess the most refined senses and the largest brains and be most capable of evolving into a dinosaur equivalent of man. Their man-like model known as the 'Dinosauroid', is pure speculation, but has aroused a great deal of public interest at the National Museum in Ottawa where it is displayed.

Below left: *Stenonychosaurus*
This dinosaur has a relatively large brain and has been credited as the most intelligent dinosaur. The brain was probably mainly concerned with its highly developed senses, fine control of its limbs and fast reflexes.
The ***Stenonychosaurus*** *had large eyes, a light body and slender, flexible fingers.*

Below: *Saurornithoides*
*Like **Stenonychosaurus**, **Saurornithoides** had a large brain and a very slender body. Its large saucer-like eyes might have been used for hunting small mammals at dusk, when other predatory dinosaurs would have been unable to see properly.*
Saurornithoides *had small sharp teeth, but these were serrated only*

*on one edge. On its foot, there was a slightly enlarged claw which was normally folded back, but which could be used to slash at potential prey. In this is resembles **Deinonychus**.*

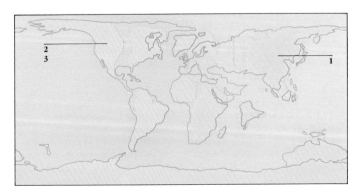

Map (right)
1 *Saurornithoides*
2 *Saurornitholestes*
3 *Stenonychosaurus*

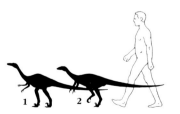

Left: *Comparative sizes*
1 *Stenonychosaurus:*
  2m (6.5ft)
2 *Saurornithoides:*
  2m (6.5ft)

DROMAEOSAURS

Pronunciation:	Drome-ee-oh-sores
Includes:	Deinonychus, Velociraptor, Dromaeosaurus
Period:	Cretaceous
	(135-70 mya)
Location:	Western North America, Britain, China

Until 1964 our knowledge of dromaeosaurs was very poor. The previous 50 years had produced just one very incomplete specimen consisting of a partial skull, lower jaws and some assorted foot bones, discovered by Barnum Brown on his travels down the Red Deer River in Alberta, Canada in 1914.

These remains were named *Dromaeosaurus* ('swift reptile'), after which the group as a whole have been named, and proved difficult to put with any particular group of theropods. The skull of this form was large and powerful, rather like that of a typical carnosaurs (page 22) and yet the foot bones were small and light as are those of typical coelurosaurs (page 12). However, 1964 saw the discovery by Grant Meyer and Professor John Ostrom, of Yale University, of a new fossil site in southern Montana. Over the next two years, this fossil site yielded the remains of a totally new and unexpected form of predatory dinosaur which was named *Deinonychus* ('terrible claw').

Deinonychus is now known from several incomplete skeletons from the early Cretaceous of Montana, which together provide

Above left: *Velociraptor*
Velociraptor can be distinguished from other dromaeosaurids by its very long and narrow head. The difference in head shape and size may well reflect differences in diet.

Above centre: *Deinonychus*
The distinctive characteristics of this dinosaur are the large head with backwardly curved teeth, the long powerful arms, and the extraordinary sickle-like second toe.

Above: *Dromaeosaurus*
Few remains of this dinosaur have been found, so this illustration is largely conjecture. It is known from skull fragments that the head has a deep, rounded snout.

a fairly detailed knowledge of the anatomy of this, and of closely related forms such as *Dromaeosaurus* and *Velociraptor*, from Mongolia.

Deinonychus is a very well known dinosaur thanks to the detailed work of Professor Ostrom, and beautifully illustrates just how sophisticated some dinosaurs were capable of being — a far cry from the typical image of the dinosaur as a useless, poorly designed, inefficient creature, destined for extinction. The skull is large, and yet light because of the large openings for the eye and the jaw muscles, and the jaws contain large, curved and serrated teeth, well suited to slicing through tough flesh. The arms and hands are long and equipped with large sharply pointed claws for gripping prey. The unusual tail is long and held stiff by special narrow bony rods and was used to balance the body, but more importantly to act as a dynamic stabiliser for rapidly moving from side to side when pursuing its prey at high speed.

Most extraordinary of all, however, is the hind leg and foot. The structures seen in this area serve to explain how all the other features fit together in the life of *Deinonychus*. The leg is quite long and slender, as befits a fast runner; but the foot is peculiarly specialised as an offensive weapon. The first toe has a short backwardly curved claw, but the second toe has an enormously enlarged vicious sickle-claw (the 'terrible claw') and the third and fourth toes are normal running toes.

How was the sickle-claw used? Undoubtedly this would have been used to slash open the soft belly of its hapless prey with vicious kicks, while the prey was held clamped by the strong and sharply taloned hands and powerful teeth. By any estimation this was a formidable killer; every aspect of its body was designed with one sole purpose — the quick and efficient killing of its prey. Even the killers of today such as the large cats (lion, jaguar, leopard, cheetah) with all their cunning and prowess would be hard pressed to better the probable killing ability of these dromaeosaurs.

Velociraptor ('speedy killer') is from the late Cretaceous of Mongolia; it differs from *Deinonychus* in the narrowness of its snout and its smaller size. Known from remains since 1924, it was only recently realised that this too was a dromaeosaur with a remarkable sickle-claw. In 1971 a Polish-Mongolian expedition to the Gobi Desert uncovered a truly remarkable fossil: the remains of *Protoceratops* and *Velociraptor* preserved as though in combat, with *Velociraptor* clutching at the head of *Protoceratops* with its hands and feet.

Right: *Deinonychus foot and claw*
The second toe, with its enormous claw, is the most striking feature of this foot. The enlarged joints allow the toe to be raised upward and backward to avoid damage while running.

Terrible claw

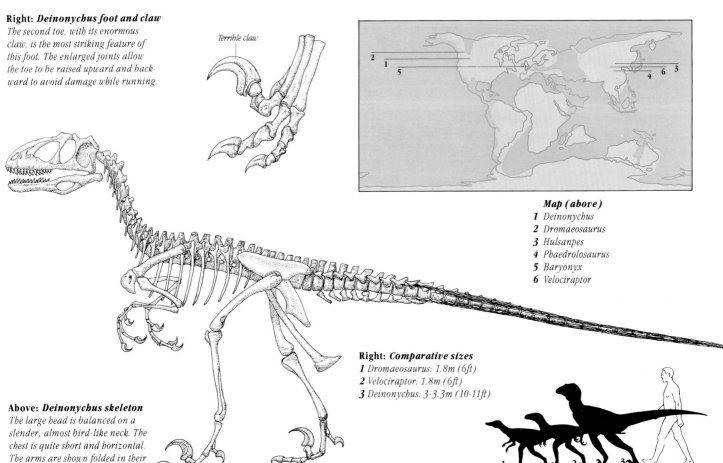

Map (above)
1 Deinonychus
2 Dromaeosaurus
3 Hulsanpes
4 Phaedrolosaurus
5 Baryonyx
6 Velociraptor

Above: *Deinonychus skeleton*
The large head is balanced on a slender, almost bird-like neck. The chest is quite short and horizontal. The arms are shown folded in their resting position.

Right: *Comparative sizes*
1 *Dromaeosaurus: 1.8m (6ft)*
2 *Velociraptor: 1.8m (6ft)*
3 *Deinonychus: 3-3.3m (10-11ft)*

CARNOSAURS

This is a grouping of theropods of decidedly mixed parentage, as in the case of the coelurosaurs (page 12). As a rule they differ markedly in body proportions from the various theropods described so far. Carnosaurs are typically large (60 metres (20 ft) or more in length) and heavily built, with strong and thick legs to carry the heavy body, rather short and apparently feeble arms and hands, and very large heads perched upon powerfully muscled necks. Despite the fact that palaeontologists have worked on these types of dinosaurs for well over 140 years, there is still little agreement over the degree to which many of the types of

theropod, included within the carnosaurs, are related. And, as will be seen below, new finds seem simply to add to the general confusion rather than clarifying things!

Allosaurus ('strange reptile') has in many ways a *strange* beginning. The first remains of this animal consisted of a single broken tail bone discovered in 1869 in late Jurassic rocks in Colorado; this bone was named *Poicilopleuron*, a little later the name was changed to *Antrodemus*. Later still in 1877, and elsewhere in Colorado, the partial skeleton was discovered of a large carnosaur, which was named *Allosaurus* and this was followed in 1883 by the discovery

Pronunciation:	Car-no-sores
Includes:	Allosaurus, Ceratosaurus, Dilophosaurus, Yangchuanosaurus, Baryonyx
Period:	Late Jurassic (150-135 mya)
Location:	Western North America, western Europe, north Africa, China

Below centre: *Ceratosaurus*
The striking feature of this dinosaur is the sizeable bony lump on its snout, similar to a rhinoceros horn.

Below right: *Dilophosaurus*
This large dinosaur had a distinctive crest on its head made from two thin wedges of bone situated side by side.

Above left: *Allosaurus*
The skull of this large carnivore could be 90cm (3ft) long. The jaws were lined with dagger-like teeth which had serrated edges back and front. ***Allosaurus*** had strong claws on its hands and feet to hold prey.

Left: *Comparative sizes*
1 *Ceratosaurus*: 6m (20ft)
2 *Dilophosaurus*: 6m (20ft)
3 *Allosaurus*: 12m (39ft)

of an almost complete skeleton. Despite all this early confusion, the name which has become generally accepted for this dinosaur is *Allosaurus* although even today occasional reference may be made to *Antrodemus*.

The skull of *Allosaurus* is very large (up to a metre (3 ft) long) and the jaws are lined with a formidable row of large, serrated teeth. Despite its large size, the skull is surprisingly light, with large spaces for muscles, eyes and nose being separated off by narrow strips of bone; this reduced the weight of the skull and made it more manageable for the animal. Another, and slightly curious feature, is the fact that there are knobs and ridges above the eye, which may have been used as signalling devices for mating (see *hadrosaurs*, page 40-43).

Ceratosaurus ('horned reptile') was discovered in 1883 at the same quarry in Colorado where the first good skeleton of *Allosaurus* was found. Although smaller than *Allosaurus*, reaching a maximum length of some 6 metres (20 ft), *Ceratosaurus* is no less interesting. In its general proportions *Ceratosaurus* is a typical carnosaur. The skull is large, and has similar eye ridges to the ones seen in *Allosaurus*; however, it does have a remarkable horn on the snout. Another more subtle difference can be seen in the hand. *Allosaurus* has a three fingered hand, whereas *Ceratosaurus* has four fingers.

Dilophosaurus ('two crested reptile') is from the early Jurassic of Arizona and appears to have grown to about the same size as *Ceratosaurus*. At first this was described as a new species of *Megalosaurus*, but later it was realised that this dinosaur had a most unusual feature: the pair of thin bony crests running along the top of the head.

Carnosaurs are likely to have been powerful predatory animals. The huge jaws lined with rows of sharp stabbing and cutting teeth clearly testify to this. Add to this the powerful neck and back and you have an animal capable of biting huge chunks of meat from their prey. What they fed on and how is not so clear. Clearly these animals were not designed for fast pursuit, as were the smaller and more agile coelurosaurs; their prey were undoubtedly larger and slower moving, whom they could either track or ambush.

Yangchuanosaurus is a newly described carnosaur based on a nearly complete skeleton from Sichuan Province, China; it bears a striking similarity to *Allosaurus*. Even newer than that is *Baryonyx* from the early Cretaceous period of Britain, a large, heavy-clawed carnosaur-like theropod which, some believe, may have had a diet of fish.

Above: *These superb exhibits from the Los Angeles County Museum show an* **Allosaurus** *attacking* **Camptosaurus**. *This shows clearly how massive the skull is and how the window-like openings in it save weight.*

Below: *Allosaurus skull*
This skull has very large jaws which bear many long curved, serrated teeth. However, the rest of the skull is lightly built with several fenestrae or windows.

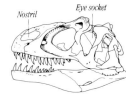

Nostril   Eye socket

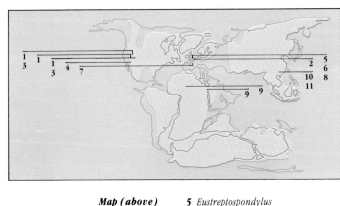

Map (above)
1 *Allosaurus*
2 *Altispinax*
3 *Ceratosaurus*
4 *Dilophosaurus*
5 *Eustreptospondylus*
6 *Megalosaurus*
7 *Priveteausaurus*
8 *Proceratosaurus*
9 *Spinosaurus*
10 *Szechuanosaurus*
11 *Yangchuanosaurus*

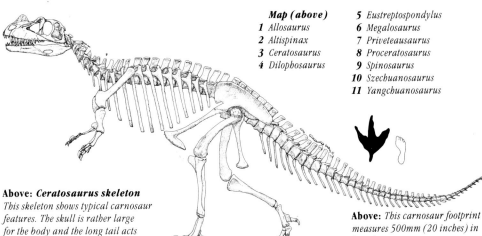

Above: *Ceratosaurus skeleton*
This skeleton shows typical carnosaur features. The skull is rather large for the body and the long tail acts as a counterbalance.

Above: *This carnosaur footprint measures 500mm (20 inches) in length.*

TYRANNOSAURIDS

Tyrannosaurids are perhaps the most well known, as well as being the largest of all theropod dinosaurs. The family Tyrannosauridae comes from *Tyrannosaurus rex*, which is far and away the best known of all dinosaurs. It is a curious fact that tyrannosaurs and their allies were not recognised as anything particularly special when they were first discovered. However, the first remains which were collected in the 1850s in rocks of latest Cretaceous age were of teeth and, large though these were, there was no way of knowing at that time precisely what the original owners of the teeth looked like. In fact it took over 50 years to discover what sort of animal these teeth belonged to. In 1902 a partial skeleton of the first *Tyrannosaurus* was discovered in Dawson County, Montana, and then another was discovered in Wyoming, all of which allowed

Henry Fairfield Osborn (a famous American palaeontologist) to describe the appearance of this new dinosaur in some detail. Since that time a little more material of *Tyrannosaurus* has been discovered and several other tyrannosaurs have come to light, the best known of which are *Tarbosaurus, Albertosaurus* and *Daspletosaurus*.

The largest specimens of *Tyrannosaurus* ('tyrant reptile') suggest that this dinosaur grew to as much as 14 metres (46 ft) in length, a little larger than the biggest of the late Jurassic theropods such as *Allosaurus*. It was clearly designed to be a devastating killing machine. The skull is very large, up to 1.3 metres (4 ft) long, extremely heavy and the jaws were lined with long, curved and serrated teeth; in addition, the neck and backbone are extremely powerful. All this points to the fact that *Tyrannosaurus*

Pronunciation:	Tie-ran-oh-sore-ids
Includes:	Tyrannosaurus, Daspletosaurus, Albertosaurus, Tarbosaurus, (other possibles: Alectrosaurus, Alioramus, Genyodectes, Indosuchus, Itemirus, Labocania, Prodeinodon, Unquillosaurus)
Period:	Latest Cretaceous (74-54 mya)
Location:	Western North America, Asia (also possibly in South America and India)

Left: *Tyrannosaurus*
This famous dinosaur, 14m (46ft) long, was the biggest carnivorous dinosaur. It might have hunted its prey actively, but it probably lived by scavenging as well. It is hard to imagine an animal of this size running down its prey.

Above: *Daspletosaurus*
It has been suggested that this dinosaur fed on quadrupedal armoured ceratopids. This would explain the need for its strong jaws and dagger-like teeth.

Above centre: *Albertosaurus*
This tyrannosaurid would have killed its prey with a strong bone-crushing bite. In addition, its sharply clawed hind foot would have delivered a fierce and disabling kick.

would have attacked its prey in a devastating rush, taking a huge bite into the side of its victim. Once clamped between the powerful jaws the prey would have been shaken violently until dead. The powerful back legs, with their sharp claws, would have been used to help to tear the prey apart, or to hold it down while huge chunks were torn off between the jaws.

Quite what the front legs were used for while all this was going on is uncertain. They could not have been used to assist in feeding because they were too short to reach the mouth, and did not have particularly sharp claws. It has been suggested that they may have been used as grapples, to hold on to a partner whilst mating. However another rather interesting, and possibly complementary, suggestion is that

they were used literally as short props to help tyrannosaurs to lift themselves off the ground, after they had been lying down.

Other tyrannosaurs include two other North American forms: *Albertosaurus* ('reptile from Alberta'), a slightly smaller and more lightly built type, and *Daspletosaurus* ('flesh eating reptile'), a much heavier version which may have tackled larger prey. *Tarbosaurus* ('reptile from Mongolia') comes from the Gobi Desert of Mongolia and is extremely similar to *Tyrannosaurus*.

Map (right)

1 *Albertosaurus*	**7** *Itemirus*
2 *Alectrosaurus*	**8** *Labocania*
3 *Alioramus*	**9** *Prodeinodon*
4 *Daspletosaurus*	**10** *Tarbosaurus*
5 *Genyodectes*	**11** *Tyrannosaurus*
6 *Indosuchus*	**12** *Unquillosaurus*

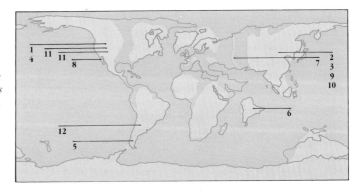

Right: *This view of **Albertosaurus** allows us to see particularly well the tiny forelimbs that are characteristic of tyrannosaurids.*

Right: *Tarbosaurus hand and foot* This two-fingered hand is quite feeble. The foot (far right) is much stronger with sharp, curved claws.

Wrist — Ankle joint —

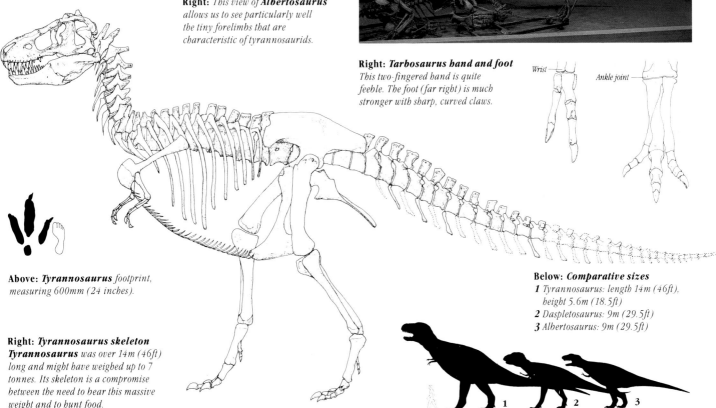

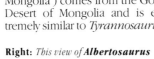

Above: *Tyrannosaurus footprint, measuring 600mm (24 inches).*

Right: *Tyrannosaurus skeleton* *Tyrannosaurus* was over 14m (46ft) long and might have weighed up to 7 tonnes. Its skeleton is a compromise between the need to bear this massive weight and to hunt food.

Below: *Comparative sizes*
1 *Tyrannosaurus: length 14m (46ft), height 5.6m (18.5ft)*
2 *Daspletosaurus: 9m (29.5ft)*
3 *Albertosaurus: 9m (29.5ft)*

PROSAUROPODS

Pronunciation:	Pro-sore-oh-pods
Includes:	Plateosaurus, Anchisaurus, Massospondylus, Lufengosaurus, Coloradia, Mussaurus, etc
Period:	Late Triassic and early Jurassic (210-190 mya)
Location:	All continents (except Antarctica, India, Australia)

These types of dinosaurs are only found in the late Triassic and earliest Jurassic rocks, right at the beginning of the reign of dinosaurs. They represent another branch of saurischian dinosaurs which are predominantly herbivorous, as opposed to the carnivorous theropods which we have seen so far. They were very important in an evolutionary sense, because they were among the first groups of dinosaurs to take to a diet of plants. Their descendants appear to be the giant sauropod dinosaurs (pages 28-33), with whom they share some similarity in body form. Prosauropods are found practically worldwide, the only notable exceptions being Australia, India and Antarctica.

Plateosaurus ('flat reptile') is probably the best known of all prosauropods, and comes from the late Triassic rocks of western Europe. It is particularly well known because remains of this dinosaur have been found in what appear to be mass graves at Trossingen (West Germany), Halberstadt (East Germany) and La Chassagne (France). The very first remains were found in Germany and were described in the 1830s, but these were very fragmentary bits and pieces. It was not until just before and after the second world war that extensive excavations at Trossingen revealed many complete skeletons, all buried together. These formed the subject of work by Friedrich Freiherr Von Huene of the University of Tubingen.

The largest *Plateosaurus* seems to be 8 metres (27 ft) in length. The head is quite small and perched on the end of a moderately long neck. Its teeth are small, peg-like and flattened from side to side, and their edges are marked by a row of rough projections (serrations); these seem to be ideal for tearing through plant tissues. The remainder of the body is quite heavily built, and the belly region is large to accommodate a large stomach, which is essential for an animal with a diet of plants. The front legs have very powerful hands, the three inner fingers of which have sharp claws and were probably used for defence; the joints between the bones of the hand are also very

Right: *Plateosaurus*
This was the first large dinosaur and fed on plants at ground level and on leaves of tall trees which it could reach by standing on its hind legs.

Far right: *Anchisaurus*
*One of the smaller prosauropods, **Anchisaurus** was another successful early herbivore. It had blunt pencil-shaped teeth spaced out along its jaw. This dinosaur was lightly built and agile, enabling it to escape from contemporary theropod predators.*

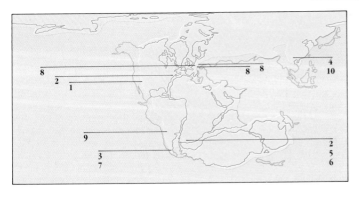

Map (above)

1 Ammosaurus	6 Melanorosaurus
2 Anchisaurus	7 Mussaurus
3 Coloradia	8 Plateosaurus
4 Lufengosaurus	9 Riojasaurus
5 Massospondylus	10 Yunnanosaurus

flexible and allow the hand to be used for walking on (see illustration). The long, heavy and muscular tail counterbalanced the animal so that it was capable of walking either in an upright position or on all fours.

The mass graves of *Plateosaurus* are something of a mystery, but do seem to point to the fact that *Plateosaurus* was an extremely abundant animal in the late Triassic and may even have lived in herds. The mass graves may well represent mem-

Above: *A side view of the skull of a* **Massospondylus** *excavated in South Africa. This was one of the most widespread dinosaurs here in late Triassic and early Jurassic times.*

bers of herds which had fallen victim to flash floods.

Other prosauropods include such forms as the North American *Anchisaurus*, a much more slenderly proportioned creature than *Plateosaurus*; *Coloradia* from South America; *Massospondylus* from southern Africa and *Lufengosaurus* from southern China. One remarkable little prosauropod called *Mussaurus* ('mouse reptile') from Patagonia is a mere 20 centimetres (8 ins) long, but this is a juvenile.

Above: **Comparative sizes**
1 *Anchisaurus: 2.5m (8.2ft)*
2 *Plateosaurus: 6·8m (20·26ft)*

Above: *The South African Museum's cast of a* **Massospondylus** *skeleton. This photo emphasises the small size of the dinosaur's head in relation to its body.*

Ring of bones supporting eye

Depressed jaw hinge

Above: **Plateosaurus skull**
This robust skull has a jaw hinge lower than the row of teeth — a feature often found in herbivores.

Right: **Plateosaurus skeleton**
This large anchisaurid has been collected from over 50 locations in Europe.

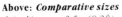

Above: **Prosauropod** *footprints, each measuring 450mm (18 inches).*

DIPLODOCIDS

Pronunciation:	Di-plod-oh-sids
Includes:	Diplodocus, Apatosaurus, Dicraeosaurus, Nemegtosaurus, Antarctosaurus
Period:	Late Jurassic to end of Cretaceous (145-64 mya)
Location:	Worldwide (except India, Australia and Antarctica)

Below: *Apatosaurus*
A large sauropod, ***Apatosaurus*** *weighed about 30 tonnes, with a thick neck and small head. It fed on low-lying vegetation around lakes and on the leaves of tall trees. It snipped these off with its peg-like teeth and swallowed them whole.*

Below right: *Diplodocus*
A close relative of ***Apatosaurus****,* ***Diplodocus*** *weighed 10-11 tonnes. Its limbs were pillar-like to support its great weight. Most of the toe nails on the front feet were small hooves, except for the inner toes which had long claws for self-defence.*

Diplodocids are among the best known of all dinosaurs. They are spectacularly large, and casts or original skeletons form the centrepiece of many of the larger museum displays around the world. These dinosaurs succeeded the prosauropods in the later Jurassic period. All of these long necked and long tailed dinosaurs are known collectively as sauropods (more examples can be seen on pages 30-33), but these are separated off as diplodocids because they all bear a family resemblance to *Diplodocus*, after which the group was named. Two of

Above: *These large* **Diplodocid** *footprints each measure 1000mm (39 inches).*

28

the best known diplodocids are *Diplodocus* and *Apatosaurus*, both of which come from late Jurassic rocks of western North America.

Apatosaurus ('deceptive reptile'), although known today from a magnificent skeleton excavated from a quarry at Dinosaur National Monument in Utah, USA in the early years of this century, has been the subject of much confusion in past years. For many years this dinosaur was called 'Brontosaurus', because of confusion over the first scrappy remains discovered in the late years of the nineteenth century. In addition, the skeleton and drawings of the skeleton always showed this dinosaur with a

head shaped rather like the one seen on the sauropod *Camarasaurus* (page 31). It was not until 1975 that things were corrected. It was then shown to everyone's satisfaction that the head of *Apatosaurus* was very like that of *Diplodocus*.

The head of *Apatosaurus* is small compared to the rest of the body, and all the teeth are grouped together across the front of the mouth—rather like a row of pencils. It seems likely that the very long neck was used like a crane jib to lift the head high into the tree tops so that it could rake in large quantities of vegetation. No chewing occurred in the mouth (it had no chewing teeth); all the plant food would have

been passed down the gullet to the stomach. The stomachs of these animals were probably built as a gigantic fermentation chamber in which all the plant material was gradually digested. To speed up digestion it seems that these dinosaurs also had a gizzard (a strong muscular chamber near the stomach), or something similar, which was lined with pebbles. Tough pieces of plant could be passed into the gizzard to be pounded up by the stones. All this would have needed strong legs and back to carry the weight, and indeed the legs are stout and pillar-like and the back bone is very strong. The tail is long and powerful, but at the end becomes very long and extremely thin. In

fact, this would seem to be a defensive weapon. The tail formed a thin whiplash to be slashed across the face of attacking theropods, such as *Allosaurus*.

Other diplodocids include *Diplodocus*, which differs very little from *Apatosaurus* apart from being longer and very much lighter in build. *Dicraeosaurus* comes from Tanzania, and is similar but a little smaller than either *Apatosaurus* or *Diplodocus*. *Nemegtosaurus*, from the Nemegt Basin of Mongolia, is only known by its skull, found in late Cretaceous rocks, which has obvious similarities to other diplodocids. This indicates that this group survived much of the age of dinosaurs.

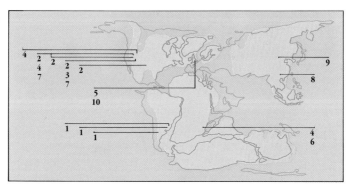

Map (left)
1 *Antarctosaurus*
2 *Apatosaurus*
3 *Atlantosaurus*
4 *Barosaurus*
5 *Cetiosauriscus*
6 *Dicraeosaurus*
7 *Diplodocus*
8 *Mamenchisaurus*
9 *Nemegtosaurus*
10 *Un-named diplodocid*

Below: *Diplodocus skeleton*
*This skeleton has the hallmarks of the diplodocids: the very small head, the long, slender neck and the long tail. This skeleton is very similar to that of **Apatosaurus**, although considerably lighter. Both the front and back legs and the pelvic girdles were extremely strong to bear the animal's weight.*

Right: *Diplodocus skull*
Here the features of diplodocids are seen clearly. Note the large eye socket and fine pencil-like teeth.

Right: *Diplodocus hand*
This hand is broad and rather short. The first finger bore a large curved claw, while the others were finished with a pad of horn.

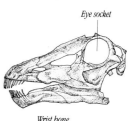

Eye socket

Wrist bone

Claw

Below: *Comparative sizes*
1 *Apatosaurus: 21m (69ft)*
2 *Diplodocus: 27m (88.5ft)*

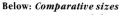

CAMARASAURS & BRACHIOSAURS

<table>
<tr><td>Pronunciation:</td><td>Cam-are-a-sores
Brak-ee-oh-sores</td></tr>
<tr><td>Includes:</td><td>Camarasaurus, Euhelopus,
Opisthocoelicaudia (?), Brachiosaurus,
Rebbachisaurus, Supersaurus, Ultrasaurus,
Pelorosaurus</td></tr>
<tr><td>Period:</td><td>Late Jurassic to early Cretaceous
(145-120 mya)</td></tr>
<tr><td>Location:</td><td>North America, Africa, Europe</td></tr>
</table>

Right: *Brachiosaurus*
The most obvious feature of this massive creature is the length of its neck, and also of its forelimbs which were longer than its hindlimbs — an unusual characteristic of these dinosaurs. Both features appear to be adaptations for feeding on foliage at the top of tall trees.

These two groups of dinosaurs seem to be quite closely related (especially when compared to other groups, such as the diplodocids), even though outwardly they look very different. Neither of these types of dinosaur have the long whiplash tail which is so characteristic of diplodocids.

Camarasaurus ('chambered reptile') remains have been discovered in late Jurassic rocks in western North America (Colorado, Wyoming and Utah), and as in the case of *Apatosaurus* (page 28), there was much confusion over both the appearance and name of this dinosaur; it has in the past been called 'Morosaurus', 'Caulodon', and 'Uintasaurus'. All was made much clearer in 1925 when a beautifully preserved, almost complete skeleton of a young *Camarasaurus* was described; it had been discovered

Left: *Comparative sizes*
1 Camarasaurus: 18m (59ft)
2 Brachiosaurus: length 22.5m (74ft);
height 12m (39ft)

Above: *Camarasaurus*
*This long sauropod is similar in general build to **Brachiosaurus**, but rather smaller. **Camarasaurus** has a short skull with a blunt snout. The nostrils are placed high on the head, just in front of the eyes, and it was once thought that this indicated that*

sauropods lived underwater with just the tops of their heads showing. The body is held horizontally as the fore and hindlimbs are almost the same length. The short neck means it would have been limited to eating from the lower branches of trees and ground level plants.

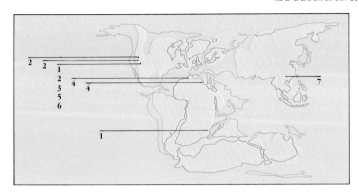

Map (above)

1	Brachiosaurus	**3** Haplocanthosaurus
2	Camarasaurus	**4** Rebbachisaurus
		5 Supersaurus
		6 Ultrasaurus
		7 Zigongosaurus

at Dinosaur National Monument in Utah, and so little was missing that it must have been a young animal that had slipped into a large river, drowned and then been buried very rapidly in river sands before any animals were able to scavenge the carcass.

From odd bones that have been found, it seems that the adult *Camarasaurus* may have reached a length of about 18 metres (60 ft), but the young one from Utah was a mere 6 metres (18ft) long. Compared to diplodocids, the neck and tail are much shorter, although the legs and chest are very similar. The main difference, however, lies in the head; this is much deeper and more powerfully built. The nostrils are very large and positioned near the front of the snout, and the jaws are much more powerful, with a long row of large, chisel-shaped teeth.

Camarasaurs seem to have been shorter and sturdier animals altogether than diplodocids, and judging from the structure of the head, they probably had a very different diet. The teeth and jaws are powerful and well able to bite off pieces of vegetation (rather than dragging leaves into the mouth like a rake, as did diplodocids) and this certainly points to a different sort of diet.

Brachiosaurus ('arm reptile') comes from Tanzania and western North America, and is found in rocks of late Jurassic age. The best example known to date comes from Tanzania and was collected by a team of scientists and African labourers in the early years of this century. It is now on display in the Natural History Museum in East Berlin, and is over 23 metres (75 ft) long (not quite as long as *Diplodocus*), but stands some 12 metres (39 ft) above the ground. It has the proportions of a gigantic giraffe, and indeed it is thought that it probably was the dinosaur equivalent of a giraffe. The exceptional length of its arms (which gave the dinosaur its name), combined with the length of the neck gave the dinosaur an enormous height advantage for reaching the highest foliage in the tallest trees.

In recent years several new brachiosaurs have been reported including *Supersaurus* and *Ultrasaurus*, but at present, even though they seem to be even larger than *Brachiosaurus*, they are not known in great detail.

Right: *This skeleton of **Brachiosaurus** is in the Humboldt Museum, Berlin. Discovered in Tanzania, it is the largest mounted dinosaur skeleton in the world. Note the length of its forelimbs.*

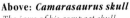

Nasal cavity · Eye socket · Chisel-like teeth

Above: *Camarasaurus skull*
The jaws of his compact skull support a closely packed array of chisel-like teeth. The large opening at the front of the skull is for the nostrils. Immediately behind the nostril is the eye socket.

Right: *Brachiosaurus skeleton*
The similarity between this skeleton and a giraffe is quite striking with the long front legs lifting the shoulders above the hips and the neck raising the head to over 13m (42ft). Muscles were attached to the spines on the neck to raise the head.

MISCELLANEOUS SAUROPODS

It is an unfortunate fact that even though there are several sauropods which are known from complete, or nearly complete, skeletons, the vast majority of fossil remains of these creatures consist of isolated bones, or partial skeletons with the vitally important pieces (especially the head) missing. As a result of this sad fact, many of the names of such sauropods have to be seen to be of dubious value because we cannot be sure of the exact anatomy of the creatures and, equally important, how they are related to one another. For example, it may be impossible to show that any of these sauropods is at all closely related to the groups already described (diplodocids, brachiosaurids and camarasaurids).

A few representatives of these sorts of sauropods are reconstructed here, but even though three dinosaurs are illustrated, and therefore give the impression of being well known, they are in fact largely guesswork. The exact number of toes and claws is unknown, the lengths of the tail and neck are mostly guessed and the structure of the head in all three is unfortunately completely unknown.

Vulcanodon (fire tooth) comes from the early Jurassic of Zimbabwe and consists of much of the rear part of a large sauropod 6 metres (20 ft) long. It seems to have been built much like a typical sauropod, with a heavy body and limbs, and comparison has been made with a better known form *Barapasaurus* from the Middle Jurassic of India. *Vulcanodon* must have lived at the same time as the lighter built prosauropods, but presumably filled a different ecological niche — perhaps feeding in different ways upon different sorts of vegetation than contemporary prosauropods.

Saltasaurus (reptile from Salta Province, Argentina) is one of the most surprising finds of the last decade. It was described by José Bonaparte and Jaime Powell in 1980, and comes from rocks of late Cretaceous age. Although incomplete, the skeleton does seem to show that the skin had embedded in it a mixture of large and small knobbly bones, which must have formed a kind of armoured protection over the back and flanks of the animal. This was so unexpected that for a long time these curious bits of bone were thought to belong to some sort of armoured ornithischian dinosaur such as an ankylosaurid (page 58). Now that this has been recognised as sauropod armour, other types may well come to light (such as *Laplatasaurus*).

Opisthocoelicaudia (posterior cavity tail) is known from a magnificent body and tail found in the late Cretaceous rocks of Mongolia. It is a relatively recent discovery (1965), following joint Polish-Mongolian expeditions to remote areas of Mongolia. Unfortunately no head or neck was found with the skeleton, but the body and limbs are very heavily built. The tail is unusually short by most sauropod standards, and it has been suggested that it may have been used as a prop for rearing up into the higher trees. Another sauropod *Nemegtosaurus* was found in rocks of similar age in Mongolia, but this is known only from the skull (page 29) and, tempting though it is, we have no way of knowing if one belonged to the other.

Other very interesting sauropods include *Omeisaurus, Datousaurus* and *Shunosaurus* from China, only recently identified from several well preserved skeletons, but not yet fully studied. The British forms of sauropods include *Ornithopsis* and *Cetiosauriscus* which are still not well known.

Right: *Vulcanodon*
This illustration shows what we think the sauropods of the early Jurassic looked like. This animal is shown with a bulky body and pillar-like legs, based on current knowledge **Barapasaurus** *probably looked similar.*

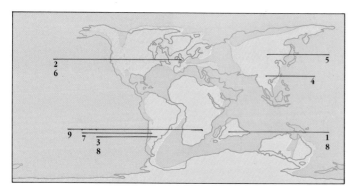

Map (left)
1 Barapasaurus
2 Cetiosauriscus
3 Laplatasaurus
4 Omeisaurus
5 Opisthocoelicaudia
6 Ornithopsis
7 Saltasaurus
8 Titanosaurus
9 Vulcanodon

Right: *Comparative sizes*
1 Opisthocoelicaudia: 12m (39ft)
2 Saltasaurus: 12m (39ft)
3 Vulcanodon: 6.5m (21ft)

Below: *Saltasaurus*
Saltasaurus, *quite a recent discovery, is of great interest because it shows that some sauropods bore bony armour. Large round plates of bone are scattered across the hide* and between them lie masses of small nodules. As shown, the tail was flexible and could have supported the body when **Saltasaurus** reared on its back legs in its efforts to obtain food.

Left: *Opisthocoelicaudia skeleton*
This dinosaur is only known from its headless skeleton. The tail has extremely unusual ball and socket joints between the vertebrae.

Nostril

Eye socket

Opening for jaw muscles

Left: *Omeisaurus skull*
This wedge-shaped skull is unusual when compared to other sauropod skulls as the nostrils are much nearer the front of the snout than in other sauropods.

Below: *While the sheer size of these animals rendered them almost immune from attack by carnivorous predators, the large claw on the inner toe of the front foot could be used as a formidable defensive weapon when the sauropod reared onto its hind legs.*

1

2

3

Above: *Opisthocoelicaudia* *In its general body proportions, this dinosaur resembles* **Camarasaurus**, *but it does have a number of peculiarities. The pillar-like legs support a bulky body, the tail is held out straight and the shoulders are quite high. Unfortunately the head and neck are unknown.*

FABROSAURS, SCUTELLOSAURUS & HETERODONTOSAURS

These are among the earliest of known ornithischian dinosaurs, their remains having been collected from rocks of very early Jurassic age (200 million years old). As described earlier, all ornithischian dinosaurs were herbivorous, and one of the most characteristic features (which can be seen in the lifelike restorations below) is the small horn-covered beak on the tip of the lower jaw. The horny beak covered a small triangular and toothless bone known as the *predentary* (see skull drawings). There are other special features, such as the palpebral bone in the eye, the shape of the pelvic bones, and the presence of bony rods lying alongside the spines of the backbone, all of which can be seen in the skeletal drawings of *Heterodontosaurus*, but these are of course invisible in the flesh restorations.

As was the case with saurischian dinosaurs, there are a number of clearly distinct groups of ornithischian: ornithopods, ceratopians, pachycephalosaurs, stegosaurs and ankylosaurs. The first groups that we shall be looking at are the ornithopods — a group which are abundant and found throughout the reign of the dinosaurs. However, the very early types, such as those discussed here, do not fall so clearly into the neat categories listed above, probably because they are so early in the history of the groups as a whole they may represent some of the types from which the later groups evolved.

Fabrosaurs include types such as *Lesothosaurus* (reptile from Lesotho), of which there are several partial skeletons known. *Lesothosaurus* has been found

Pronunciation:	Fah-bro-sores
	Het-er-oh-dont-oh-sores
	Skew-tell-oh-sore-us
Includes:	Heterodontosaurus, Lesothosaurus,
	Scutellosaurus, Echinodon, Alocodon,
	Geranosaurus, Abrictosaurus, Trimucrodon,
	Gongbusaurus, Lanasaurus, Nanosaurus
Period:	Early Jurassic to early Cretaceous
	(200-114 mya)
Location:	USA, southern Africa, China, western Europe

Left: *Heterodontosaurus*
This dinosaur has three different types of teeth: sharp cutting ones at the front, fangs behind these, and broad teeth at the sides.

Below: *Lesothosaurus*
This small ornithopod was a lightly built bipedal form that could probably run fast to avoid predators.

Below: *Comparative sizes*
1 *Lesothosaurus:*
   90cm (35in)
2 *Heterodontosaurus:*
   120cm (47in)
3 *Scutellosaurus:*
   134cm (53in)

Left: *Scutellosaurus*
A close relative of **Lesothosaurus**, **Scutellosaurus** *was distinguished by being covered with bony plates set into the skin, and by the extreme length of its tail.*

in southern Africa and is a small creature 1 metre (3 ft) long. It has graceful proportions and long, slender back legs, all of which indicate that these were agile, fast moving animals. Although they lack the grasping hands of theropods, they tend to resemble small theropods (page 12) in their general proportions and appearance. Alert and fast moving, these animals were well adapted to evade the smaller early carnivorous dinosaurs which lived at the same time. This dinosaur was clearly a forerunner of the ornithopods (see pages 36-43).

The narrow horny beak of these animals suggests that they may have been able to selectively nip off small tender shoots and fruits in preference to tougher, less palatable vegetation.

Heterodontosaurs are represented by *Heterodontosaurus* (mixed tooth reptile) again from southern Africa. This creature is known from several skulls and one almost complete skeleton, and appears to have been only slightly larger 1-1.5 metres (3-5 ft) than *Lesothosaurus*. Although in outward appearance these two animals are quite similar, closer inspection will show many differences. Most notable are the large grasping hands of *Heterodontosaurus*, and also the head. The head has large tusk-like teeth at the front of the jaws, and behind these a row of sharp chipping teeth.

Clearly *Heterodontosaurus*, armed with claws and tusks, was better able to defend itself than *Lesothosaurus* and was also better able to chew tough vegetation, such as the cycad frond illustrated below.

Scutellosaurus (bony plated reptile) comes from southern USA and is also of early Jurassic age. In general it is similar to *Lesothosaurus*, but this animal has a well developed bony armour on its back and sides, as well as a little on its head. It is suspected that this type is very close to the origin of the later armoured dinosaurs, the ankylosaurids (page 58).

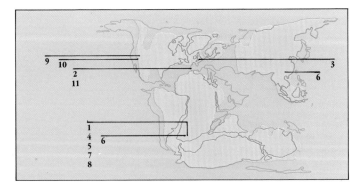

Map (above)

1 *Abrictosaurus*	**6** *Gongbusaurus*
2 *Alocodon*	**7** *Lanasaurus*
3 *Echinodon*	**8** *Lesothosaurus*
4 *Fabrosaurus*	**9** *Nanosaurus*
5 *Geranosaurus*	**10** *Scutellosaurus*
	11 *Trimucrodon*

Below: *Heterodontosaurus skull*
This shows the different types of teeth quite clearly. They may have chewed up food, rather than cropping it, by rotating the lower jaw as the mouth closed.

Below: *A side view of a* **Heterodontosaurus** *skull which was excavated from the northern slopes of Krommenspruit Mountain in South Africa. Note the tusk-like tooth and cheek teeth.*

Below: *Heterodontosaurus skeleton*
This reconstructed skeleton shows it to be a lightly built, agile animal. The long slender hind leg is a typical sign of a fleet-footed runner which presumably relied on its speed to escape from its predators. The bony rods along the backbone stiffened the back, tail and hips.

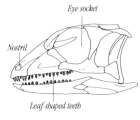

Eye socket

Nostril

Leaf-shaped teeth

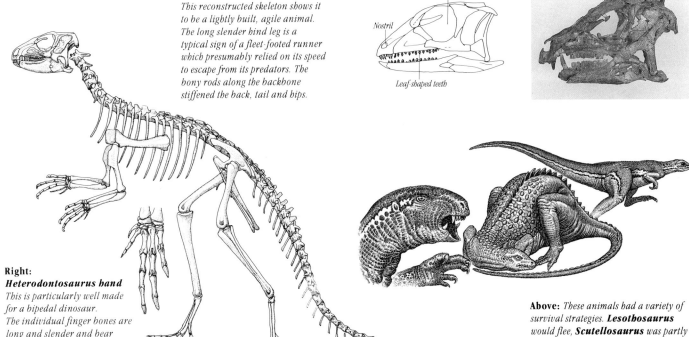

Right:
Heterodontosaurus hand
This is particularly well made for a bipedal dinosaur. The individual finger bones are long and slender and bear well developed claws. The many wrist bones suggest flexibility.

Above: *These animals had a variety of survival strategies.* **Lesothosaurus** *would flee,* **Scutellosaurus** *was partly armoured, and* **Heterodontosaurus** *was agressive when cornered.*

HYPSILOPHODONTIDS

Pronunciation:	Hip-see-loaf-oh-don-tids
Includes:	Hypsilophodon, Dryosaurus, Tenontosaurus, Xiaosaurus, Dysalotosaurus, Fulgurotherium, Loncosaurus, Othnielia, Parkosaurus, Thescelosaurus, Valdosaurus, Zephyrosaurus, Orodromeus
Period:	Late Jurassic to late Cretaceous (155-64 mya)
Location:	China, Europe, Africa, North America, Australia, possibly South America

Despite the jaw-cracking name, these ornithopods are quite simple little creatures. The name hypsilophodontid refers to the family of related dinosaurs and derives from one of the first of these dinosaurs to be discovered and described: *Hypsilophodon* (high ridged tooth). In general these types of dinosaurs are small to medium-sized 2-4 metres (6-13 ft) long and tend to be rather agile and built for speed (rather like larger versions of fabrosaurs (page 34) — with one notable exception!)

Hypsilophodon was discovered in rocks of early Cretaceous age on the sea cliffs of the Isle of Wight (southern Britain) in the middle of the last century. It comes from rocks which are the same age as those in which *Iguanodon* (pages 6-11 and 38) was found and, when first discovered, was described as a young individual of *Iguanodon* since the remains were of a dinosaur that was no more than

Right: *Tenontosaurus*
This strongly built ornithopod weighed up to 1 tonne and had a massive, powerful tail which might have been used at times to defend itself from packs of predatory *Deinonychus*.

Below: *Hypsilophodon*
One of the best known and most successful of the small ornithopods, this was a comparatively small dinosaur. It had short arms, each with five fingers, and long legs, each with four toes. Its stiff tail was used as a stabiliser.

Below: *Comparative sizes*
1 Hypsilophodon: 2m (6.6ft)
2 Dryosaurus: 3-4m (10-13ft)
3 Tenontosaurus: 4.5-6.5m (15-21ft)

Above: *Dryosaurus*
A large hypsilophodontid, *Dryosaurus* had powerful hind legs and strong arms. It had sharp ridged cheek teeth but no teeth at the front of the jaw. It probably nipped off vegetation with its bony beak.

1   2   3

2 metres (6 ft) long. Several skeletons of this dinosaur were discovered following the early finds, and now through the extensive research of Dr Peter Galton (Bridgeport, USA) we can say that it is one of the best known of all dinosaurs.

At first it was thought that *Hypsilophodon* was a small, tree-dwelling creature (living a life similar to the living tree-kangaroo of Papua New Guinea) and it is still illustrated on tree branches in some dinosaur books even today. However, it is now realised that *Hypsilophodon* was a running dinosaur first and foremost. It has the long legs and narrow feet of a runner, and the tail was held stiff by bundles of bony rods (ossified tendons),

which helped the tail to act as a dynamic stabiliser (for rapid changes of direction to throw off pursuers). *Hypsilophodon* was also well adpated to eat plants, with a sharp beak, and chewing teeth behind, as well as fleshy cheeks to hold food in the mouth while it is chewed. This feature is also to be seen in *Heterodontosaurus*, and is found in nearly all other ornithischians.

Dryosaurus has been found in late Jurassic rocks in Tanzania (East Africa), western North America and perhaps in Europe as well. Some remains of this little dinosaur were discovered in the same deposits as those from which one of the biggest of all dinosaurs (*Brachiosaurus*, page 30) was recovered. *Dryo-*

saurus was medium-sized compared with most other ornithopods, most remains are from individuals between 3 and 4 metres (10-13 ft) long. The body is short and compact, with the belly slung between the legs for better balance (made possible by the rotation of the pelvic bones found in all ornithischians). Although it appears to be very similar to *Hypsilophodon* there are several tell-tale differences: there are only three toes on the back foot (four in *Hypsilophodon*) and there are no teeth at the front of the top jaw (there are five little ones in *Hypsilophodon*).

Tenontosaurus (stiff reptile) is by far the biggest of all known hypsilophodontids, and is much

less graceful and nimble in appearance. The remains of this dinosaur were discovered many years ago by Barnum Brown, a very famous fossil collector from North America, but were not described until quite recently (1970) as a result of some new work in Montana (USA). *Tenontosaurus* comes from rocks of early Cretaceous age and appears to have reached lengths of 4-6 metres (13-20 ft). It had a stiff tail, like that of *Hypsilophodon*, and had heavy feet and limbs to support the larger and extremely heavy body.

Xiaosaurus (=*Yandusaurus*) is another new and very well preserved hypsilophodontid that has recently been described from the late Jurassic of China.

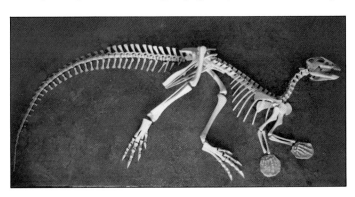

Above: *This reconstruction of an immature* **Hypsilophodon** *is based on skeletal material held in the Sandown Museum, Isle of Wight. It is made of polyester resin reinforced with fibreglass.*

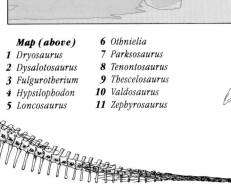

Map (above)
1 *Dryosaurus*
2 *Dysalotosaurus*
3 *Fulgurotherium*
4 *Hypsilophodon*
5 *Loncosaurus*
6 *Othnielia*
7 *Parksosaurus*
8 *Tenontosaurus*
9 *Thescelosaurus*
10 *Valdosaurus*
11 *Zephyrosaurus*

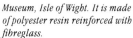

Above:
Hypsilophodon skeleton
This form was a lightly built, speedy biped. Here the hind legs show adaptations typical of running animals — all segments of the leg are elongated, particularly the upper part of the foot.

Above: **Tenontosaurus foot**
This foot, very similar to that of **Hypsilophodon***, is typical of a fast-running creature.*

Left: *This small* **Hypsilophodontid** *footprint measures only 100mm (4 inches).*

IGUANODONTS

Pronunciation:	Ig-wan-oh-donts
Includes:	Iguanodon (several species), Ouranosaurus (plus the unnamed species from Niger), Camptosaurus, possibly Muttaburrasaurus, Craspedodon, Callovosaurus, Probactrosaurus
Period:	Late Jurassic to early part of late Cretaceous (145-80 mya)
Location:	USA, western Europe, Asia, Africa, possibly Australia

Iguanodonts are ornithopod dinosaurs of generally medium to large size (tending to range between 5 and 10 metres (16-33 ft) in length) and are in many respects rather like larger versions of the hypsilophodontids seen earlier (pages 36-37). The earliest members of this family are found in rocks of late Jurassic age, and they therefore overlap the hypsilophodontids. Iguanodonts of one sort or another seem to have persisted into the latter parts of the Cretaceous period, but their time of greatest abundance and variety seems to have been the early Cretaceous, prior to the appearance of the tremendously successful duckbilled dinosaurs (hadrosaurids—pages 40-43) of the late Cretaceous. The group gets its name (as in so many cases) from one of the earliest

Right: *Muttaburrasaurus*
This Australian dinosaur had a low broad head with a heavy bony lump above the snout, and its teeth may have been used for chopping plants.

Below right: *Iguanodon*
The small hooves on its hands and feet could be used for locomotion. The large thumb spike may have been used for pulling down tree branches.

Left: *Ouranosaurus*
This spectacular ornithopod had a remarkable 'sail' along its back made from skin stretched over enlarged spines along the backbone.

Above: *Iguanodont* footprints, each measuring 500mm (20 inches)

Above: *Camptosaurus*
This is the earliest known Iguanodont and is more primitive, being smaller, lacking the spiked thumb and having an extra toe.

Right: *Comparative sizes*
1 *Camptosaurus: 5-7m (16-23ft)*
2 *Muttaburrasaurus: 7m (23ft)*
3 *Iguanodon: 10m (33ft)*

dinosaurs of this type to be described: *Iguanodon*.

Iguanodon (iguana tooth) is famous for a number of reasons. It was one of the first dinosaurs to be scientifically described and named; it was one of the founder members of Richard Owen's 'Dinosauria' in 1842, and nearly 40 years later (in 1878) a remarkable discovery of more than 30 skeletons of *Iguanodon* was made in early Cretaceous clays in a coal mine in the village of Bernissart (SW Belgium).

Iguanodon bernissartensis (the species which comes from Bernissart, but is found elsewhere in western Europe as well) was a large ornithopod, reaching lengths of 10 metres (33 ft) or more, and weighing perhaps 1.5 tonnes. This species seems to have had particularly powerful forelimbs and hooved fingers on its hands, and may well have spent some of its time walking on all fours (as seen in the skeleton reconstruction here). The hand was also remarkable because of its thumb, which has

the form of a large, sharp, conical spine; this was undoubtedly used as a fearsome stilleto-like weapon to fend off attacks by carnivorous dinosaurs. Another species of *Iguanodon* is *Iguanodon atherfieldensis* (named after a skeleton found near Atherfield Point, on the Isle of Wight, England, but also known elsewhere in Europe, including Bernissart); this is smaller 7 metres (22 ft) long and more lightly built, and as in the colour illustration, would have spent more of its time on its hindlegs. Details of a new species of *Iguanodon* from North America are emerging— the first to be based on good material from that continent, and there would appear to be a species of *Iguanodon* (or something very much like it) from Mongolia.

Camptosaurus (flexible reptile) comes from western North America and England and is found in rocks of late Jurassic age. Most skeletons of this dinosaur are medium-sized 4-6 metres (13-19 ft) in length. It

differs little from *Iguanodon*, although it does not have the well-developed thumb spine.

Ouranosaurus (brave reptile) comes from early Cretaceous rocks of Niger. Although a little smaller than the largest *Iguanodon*, at 7 metres (23 ft) long, it has an impressive row of tall spines down its back. It also has a rather broader snout (quite like those of some duckbilled dinosaurs on pages 40-43) and a pair of curious little lumps on its head. Another ornithopod, but much more heavily built than

Ouranosaurus, has also been found at Niger, and is currently being described by Dr Souad Chabli in Paris, France.

Muttaburrasaurus (reptile from Muttaburra) comes from the early Cretaceous of Australia. It is unfortunately not too well known because the skeleton is very incomplete, but appears to have been about the same size as *Ouranosaurus*. It has an unusually large hump on its nose. The precise relationship of this dinosaur with other iguanodontids is a little uncertain.

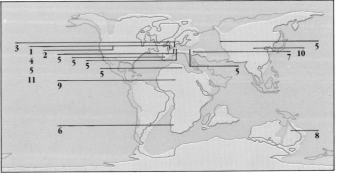

Below: ***Iguanodon hand and foot***
The hand (top) has strong hoof-like fingers and a sharp, off-set thumb. The three-toed foot (bottom) was very strong to support to weight of this large beast.

Map (above)

1 *Callovosaurus*	6 *Kangnasaurus*
2 *Camptosaurus*	7 *Mochlodon*
3 *Craspedodon*	8 *Muttaburrasaurus*
4 *Cumnoria*	9 *Ouranosaurus*
5 *Iguanodon*	10 *Probactrosaurus*
	11 *Vectisaurus*

Fused wrist bones

Thumb spike

Ankle joint

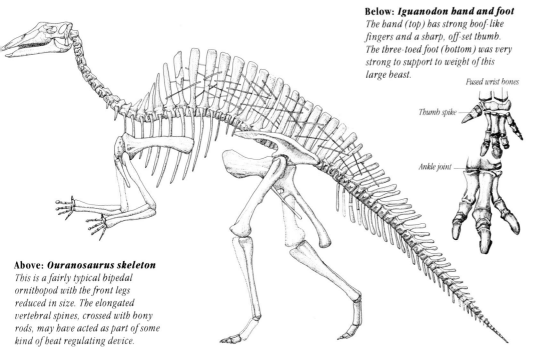

Above: ***Ouranosaurus skeleton***
This is a fairly typical bipedal ornithopod with the front legs reduced in size. The elongated vertebral spines, crossed with bony rods, may have acted as part of some kind of heat regulating device.

Above: *This skeleton cast of* ***Iguanodon*** *can be seen in Frankfurt's Senckenberg Museum.*

HADROSAURIDS I

Hadrosaurids were the last group of ornithopods to appear during the reign of dinosaurs. The earliest ones date from the middle of the Cretaceous period, and although they only lasted until the close of the Cretaceous, (the time of extinction of all dinosaurs) hadrosaurids evolved into an almost bewildering variety of forms; they also became remarkably abundant, at least as judged by the large number of fossils of these animals found in many parts of the world.

As a group, hadrosaurids grew to about the size of large iguanodontids (10 metres (33 ft) or so in length) although there are one or two exceptionally large ones known, such rare specimens of the Canadian hadrosaurid *Edmontosaurus* and the Chinese *Shantungosaurus* which are known to have reached lengths in excess of 13 metres (42 ft). As seen here, most hadrosaurids are not too dissimilar to iguanodontids in the shape and proportions of their bodies. Hadrosaurids can usually be distinguished by their broad, flattened, duck-like beak—which has given them their common name 'duck-billed dinosaurs', and the fact that there are only four digits on the hand. Hadrosaurids have dispensed with the thumb altogether; precisely why they

Pronunciation:	Had-roe-sore-ids
Includes:	Anatosaurus (=Anatotitan), Edmontosaurus Shangtungosaurus, Kritosaurus, possibly Bactrosaurus
Period:	Late Cretaceous (85-64 mya)
Location:	North America, South America, Europe, Asia

should have done away with what appears to be a rather useful defensive weapon is not at all clear. It could be that hadrosaurids simply relied on greater speed and agility to avoid being preyed upon. An alternative explanation, based on new work on these dinosaurs, suggests that they were highly sociable animals,

Right: *Bactrosaurus*
*One of the earliest hadrosaurs, **Bactrosaurus** had batteries of cheek teeth to grind up plant material.*

Below: *Anatosaurus*
This massive animal had a broad 'duck bill' mouth, used to gather up large amounts of vegetation.

Above: *Kritosaurus*
This medium-sized crestless hadrosaur had a deep narrow face with a rounded hump in front of the eyes.

Above: *Edmontosaurus*
*Closely related to **Anatosaurus**, **Edmontosaurus** had about one thousand strong teeth in the cheek region of its mouth.*

Below: *Comparative sizes*
1 *Bactrosaurus: 4-6m (13-20ft)*
2 *Kritosaurus: 9m (30ft)*
3 *Anatosaurus: 10-13m (33-42ft)*
4 *Edmontosaurus: 10-13m (33-42ft)*

living in large herds which provided considerable safety.

The hadrosaurids featured on this page are often referred to as 'hadrosaurine', or more simply as 'flat-headed hadrosaurs' — the reason for this name becomes very apparent if you turn to the next page!

Bactrosaurus (reptile from Bactria) is an early hadrosaur, from the middle Cretaceous of Mongolia. It is quite small (6 metres (19 ft) in length) and does not seem to have had a particularly broad beak. One important feature not mentioned so far about hadrosaurs is their teeth. The jaws of hadrosaurids are lined with many hundreds of small, diamond-shaped teeth, which are wedged together to form a tooth battery (see below)

and provide a powerful crushing, chewing action to break up tough plant food. *Bactrosaurus* had this same sort of jaw, which therefore makes it clearly a hadrosaurid. At the moment there is some dispute about the position of *Bactrosaurus*; it may well be an early crested hadrosaurid.

Edmontosaurus (reptile from Edmonton) is a large hadrosaurid (up to 13 metres (42 ft) long), and typical of this group. The skeleton is shown in detail below.

Anatosaurus (duck reptile) is so named because of its extraordinarily flattened, broad, duck-like bill. Broad shallow troughs around the nostrils probably housed an expandable pouch which may have been used as a resonator for making loud,

roaring sounds to attract mates, or defend territories. Because of complications over the original name, a recent suggestion has been made to rename this particular dinosaur *Anatotitan* (gigantic duck).

Kritosaurus (chosen reptile)

has a rather distinct 'Roman nose'. The shape of the nose may well have been very important for these animals since it would have affected the type of honk or bellow that they could make, which would have been an important part of their recognition system.

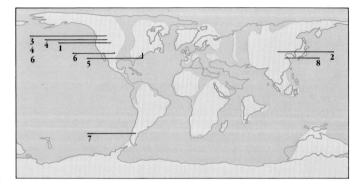

Left: *Kritosaurus skull*
Note the unusual bump on the nose of this skull.

Right: *The Royal Ontario Museum's fine panel mount of the skeleton of* **Hadrosaurus***, a dinosaur that could grow to a length of 9m (30ft). Note the rounded bump above the nostrils and the mass of bony reinforcing rods along the spine.*

Map (above)

1 Anatosaurus	3 Brachylophosaurus	6 Kritosaurus
2 Bactrosaurus	4 Edmontosaurus	7 Secernosaurus
	5 Hadrosaurus	8 Shantungosaurus

Below: *Edmontosaurus foot*
This foot is similar to that of iguanodontids. The same adaptations can be seen — compact, robust toes spreading out to support the animal's weight over a larger area.

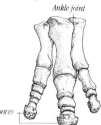

Ankle joint

Hooves

Above: *Edmontosaurus skeleton*
Similar to an iguanodontid, this had enlarged hind legs, a long tail balancing the front of the body, a flexible neck and small front legs. The bony tendons attached to the vertebral spines of the back tied the vertebrae together so the body did not sag either side of the pelvis.

Nostril opening

Eye socket

Above: **Hadrosaurid** *hind footprint, measuring 550mm (22 inches).*

HADROSAURIDS II

The other group of hadrosaurids are rather more unusual than the ones described on the previous page. They can be referred to as 'lambeosaurine' or alternatively as 'crested hadrosaurs' for obvious reasons. The name 'lambeosaurine' derives from *Lambeosaurus* — a hadrosaur with a large, helmet-like crest (very similar to that of *Corythosaurus* below). The name *Lambeosaurus* means literally 'Lambe's reptile' and was named in honour of Dr Lawrence Lambe, a Canadian palaeontologist who did a great deal of work on hadrosaurs earlier this century. Apart from the prominent headgear, there are very few obvious differences between crested and non-crested hadrosaurids. One of the few consistent differences is in the pelvis, where the ischium is far larger and heavier, and J-shaped (see below and previous page).

Although the bodies of these dinosaurs are remarkably constant, the crests on their heads are very distinctive. Some, such as *Saurolophus* and *Prosaurolophus*, have relatively low spinelike projections from the back of the cavity around the nose. *Tsintaosaurus* has previously been included with these sorts of dinosaur because it too seemed to have a spine-like crest, albeit one that pointed forward and upward (resembling nothing if not a unicorn). However, there is now considerable doubt about the reality of the spine. Others have much more substantial crests with hollow interiors and these can appear either as rather elaborate helmets or as long tubular structures (compare *Edmontosaurus* and *Corythosaurus* with *Parasaurolophus* illustrated below).

Parasaurolophus (parallel crested reptile) is perhaps the

Pronunciation:	Had-roe-sore-ids
Includes:	Tsintaosaurus, Saurolophus, Prosaurolophus, Lambeosaurus, Corythosaurus, Parasaurolophus
Period:	Late Cretaceous (80-64 mya)
Location:	Western North America, eastern Asia

Left: *Comparative sizes*
1 *Tsintaosaurus: 7m (23ft)*
2 *Saurolophus: 9-12m (30-40ft)*
3 *Corythosaurus: 10m (33ft)*
4 *Parasaurolophus: 10m (33ft)*

Right: *Parasaurolophus*
The most striking crest of all — a long tube up to 1m (3.3ft) long.

Below: *Corythosaurus*
This circular crest was filled with a complex system of breathing tubes.

Above left: *Tsintaosaurus*
This was one of the most unusual crested hadrosaurs since its crest pointed forwards. It took the form of a hollow tube which stood straight up between the eyes.

Above: *Saurolophus*
*This hadrosaur had a prominent bony ridge on top of its skull, and this ran back into a small spike. The spike's size and shape varies between the several species of **Saurolophus**.*

Above: *Hadrosaurid*
front footprint, measuring 600mm (24 inches).

most unusual of all hadrosaurids. The remains of this type of hadrosaur are unfortunately rare, and have so far only been recovered from North America. The one reasonably complete skeleton of this animal indicates an animal about 10 metres (33 ft) in length. The crest is long and tubular and can reach lengths of 1 metre (3 ft), although in others it can be considerably shorter and hooked. The hollow interior of the crest consists of a pair of looped tubes, which join the windpipe to the nostrils.

There have been a number of suggested uses for the crest in the past. For a long time it was thought that this tube acted a little like a snorkel, so that these animals could breathe while feeding on aquatic plants at the water's edge. Unfortunately this idea is not realistic because the far end of the tube is closed! Another idea, also linked with the idea that these animals lived in or around water, was that the tube acted as an air reservoir while feeding or diving. However, the volume of air held in the tubes would have been insignificant for this use. The most likely theory, and the one favoured here, is that the tubes of the crest served as resonators, rather like the pipes of a trombone, in order to produce a distinctive sound. The tubes also give the animal a very distinctive appearance which may have been important for individual recognition purposes.

Corythosaurus (Corinthian's helmet reptile) has a higher type of crest, which is similar too, if not quite so elaborate as, that of *Lambeosaurus*. Recent research suggests that male and female as well as youngsters of these types can be distinguished by the shape and proportions of the crest.

Saurolophus and *Prosaurolophus* have rather flat faces, with an upturned ridge above the eye. The whole area above the nose may well have been covered by a large inflatable pouch of skin which again acted as a resonator.

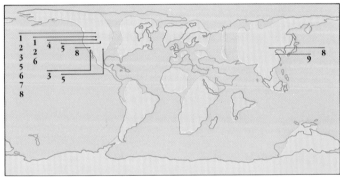

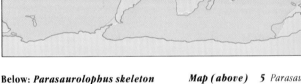

Below: *Parasaurolophus skeleton*
This skeleton is rather heavily built, especially the shoulder girdle and front leg. This dinosaur would have made good use of its front legs in walking or wading. The tail here shows the flattening typical of hadrosaurids.

Map (above)
1 *Corythosaurus*
2 *Hypacrosaurus*
3 *Lambeosaurus*
4 *Maiasaura*
5 *Parasaurolophus*
6 *Procheneosaurus*
7 *Prosaurolophus*
8 *Saurolophus*
9 *Tsintaosavrus*

Above: *Lambeosaurus* being
prepared at the Tyrrell Museum of Palaeontology, Alberta. It will be shown drinking from a pool, hence the position.

Left: *Corythosaurus crest*
These drawings show the internal anatomy of three lambeosaurine hadrosaur crests.

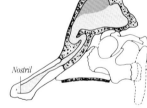

Cross section through bone

Nostril

Above: *Lambeosaurus crest*
The areas marked in red on all three crests are the nasal cavities.

Left: *Parasaurolophus crest*
The crests probably served as visual signals which allowed members of individual species to recognise one another.

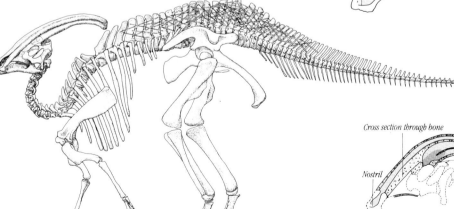

PSITTACOSAURS & PROTOCERATOPIDS

Psittacosaurs and protoceratopid dinosaurs both belong to a group of dinosaurs known more generally as ceratopians (see also pages 46-49). The ceratopians were one of the last groups of dinosaurs to appear in the Mesozoic and are found only in late Cretaceous rocks. However, even though they did appear rather late on the scene, they rapidly became extremely abundant. The really distinctive feature of all these sorts of dinosaur is the narrow, hooked beak at the front of mouth.

Psittacosaurus (parrot reptile) takes its name from the parrot-like beak which it possesses. It is a small dinosaur; none seem to attain a length of more than about 2 metres (6 ft). Most remains of this type of dinosaur come from rocks of either the latest stage of the early Cretaceous or the early part of the late Cretaceous of Mongolia and China. There is one rather doubtful specimen from the early Cretaceous of West Germany (named *Stenopelix*), which some believe to be a psittacosaur, but the remains are rather too fragmentary to allow clear identification.

The first fossils of psittacosaurs were discovered during the American Central Asiatic Expeditions of the 1920s, which went to the Mongolian People's Republic. Two quite well preserved skeletons and many other fragmentary remains were discovered, including those of baby psittacosaurs. At first the two skeletons were given different names: *Psittacosaurus* and *Protiguanodon,* but after the rock was cleared from the bones, it became clear that these were one and the same animal.

Unlike most other ceratopians, psittacosaurs were built much like the ornithopod dinosaurs featured earlier (pages 36-43). The back legs are considerably longer and stronger than the front ones and the long tail helped to counterbalance the animal, so that it could walk and run on its back legs with ease. The hands are quite large and powerful and could have been used for digging, grasping and walking when need be. The head, apart from the narrow beak, is unadorned with horns or frills as in most other ceratopians. One strange discovery was that one of the skeletons from Mongolia was preserved with a large pile of small pebbles in the area where the stomach would have been expected to be. This was no accident. The stones are otherwise known as *gastroliths* (stomach stones) and were held

Pronunciation:	Pro-toe-ser-uh-tope-ids
	Sit-ak-oh-sores
Includes:	Protoceratops, Psittacosaurus
	(=Protiguanodon), Bagaceratops, Stenopelix
Period:	Late part of early Cretaceous — late
	Cretaceous (110-64 mya)
Location:	Eastern Asia, North America, possibly Europe

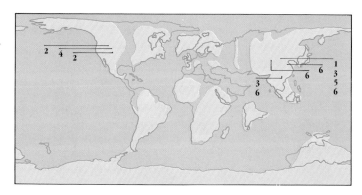

Below: *Protoceratops*
This is one of the earliest horned dinosaurs. The skull had a well developed neck shield.

Map (above)
1 Bagaceratops 4 Montanoceratops
2 Leptoceratops 5 Protoceratops
3 Microceratops 6 Psittacosaurus

Left: *This skeleton of **Psittacosaurus** is on display at the Moscow Academy of Sciences. It shows the light build of this bipedal dinosaur.*

Right: *Comparative sizes*
1 Protoceratops: 1.8m (6ft)
2 Psittacosaurus: 2m (6.6ft)

Left: *Psittacosaurus skeleton*
This form is very like the earlier bipedal ornithopods. The front legs are quite robust, however, and might well have been used for walking as well as for other tasks. The parrot-like beak shows that it is a ceratopian.

Right: *Psittacosaurus*
An important early ceratopian, this dinosaur has been considered particularly significant because it seems to show characteristics that are intermediate between ornithopods and ceratopians.

in the stomach area to grind up tough plant food.

Protoceratops (first horned face) were also fairly small dinosaurs, reaching lengths of 2 metres (6 ft). They were four footed and more heavily built creatures than psittacosaurs.

These dinosaurs were also found in Mongolia by the American Central Asiatic Expedition of the 1920s, and in considerable numbers. It has been possible to distinguish between young, old, male and female types of *Protoceratops* through careful analysis of the many skeletons, and another remarkable discovery in Mongolia, made at the same time as the skeletons, was that of a series of well preserved nests with eggs. Over 30 eggs were found in some nests, arranged in neat concentric rings, and it is thought that several female *Protoceratops* may have used the same nest to lay their eggs.

Apart from the difference in posture, *Protoceratops* had a much larger and heavier head, with a small nose horn (more prominent in the male than the female) and a large crest, or frill, on the back of the head for the attachment of powerful jaw muscles. The frill may also have been used as a signalling or warning device in their behaviour.

Below: *Protoceratops skeleton*
This moved on all-fours and the front legs are as long as the hind legs. Trellis-like bones across the vertebrae prevent the body sagging.

CERATOPIDS I

Pronunciation:	Ser-ah-tope-ids
Includes:	Triceratops, Centrosaurus, Styracosaurus, Brachyrhinoceratops, Pachyrhinosaurus, Monoclonius
Period:	Late Cretaceous (80-64 mya)
Location:	Western North America

Right: *Styracosaurus*
This had a remarkable neck frill surrounded with bone nodules at the sides and the back.

Below: *Triceratops*
The best known horned dinosaur, this had a short bone-rimmed frill and three sharp horns on the face.

The larger and in many ways more typical ceratopians were found considerably earlier than the psittacosaurs and protoceratopsids, in fact during the 1850s in the early years of the Geological Survey of North America. Unfortunately the first remains were very poorly preserved scraps of bone; the only really distinctive feature being some teeth with double roots (which is very unusual for reptiles). It was not until the late 1880s that good material was collected in late Cretaceous rocks in Wyoming (which included skulls and complete skeletons of the ceratopian *Triceratops*). Somewhat later (in the first two decades of the 20th century) more ceratopians were found in Canada, along the Red Deer River in Alberta. Since that time more ceratopians have been found in North America but, apart from the smaller protoceratopids and psittacosaurs of Asia, no large ceratopians have been recovered with certainty from any other continent.

The ceratopians chosen for this and the next sections have been divided somewhat artificially into two groups, which will be referred to respectively as the 'short frilled' and 'long frilled' types; a simple comparison of the illustrations should be sufficient to explain the differences.

Triceratops (three-horned face) is one of the best known dinosaurs, and comes from rocks which were laid down right at the end of the reign of the dinosaurs (in the latest Cretaceous).

Below: *Centrosaurus*
This medium-sized ceratopid had a single horn on its snout and small spines round the back of its neck frill. There were two curved horns on the edge of the frill pointing forwards.

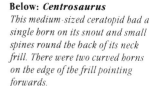

Below: *Comparative sizes*
1 *Styracosaurus:* 5.5m (18ft)
2 *Centrosaurus:* 6m (20ft)
3 *Triceratops:* 9m (29.5ft)

Left: *This fine skeleton of* **Triceratops prorsus**, *the smallest species of* **Triceratops**, *is on display at the Smithsonian Institution, Washington DC.*

The largest individuals seem to have attained a length of about 9 metres (29 ft), which is about the largest size of any ceratopian. Although not particularly large or long, by comparison with many other types of dinosaur, *Triceratops* was very powerfully built; the body was compact, with a short tail, and powerfully muscled legs, hips and shoulders; the back was strong to support the huge heads of these animals. The head is rather like an exaggerated version of that seen in *Protoceratops*, except that the horn on the nose is far larger and matched by the long brow horns, and the frill is more solid. The jaws and teeth are also far larger and more powerful.

The fearsome horns of *Triceratops* were undoubtedly used for defence, particularly against tyrannosaurids, which lived at the same time. However, it also seems probable that the horns and frill had a behavioural purpose as well. The horns may have been used as signals and weapons (for head-to-head wrestling matches between rival males), for example for establishing the leadership of herds. The frill may well have served as a deflector or shoulder shield in such contests.

Centrosaurus and *Styracosaurus* are very similar 'short frills' known mostly from north western USA and adjacent parts of Canada. Both reached about 6 metres (20 ft) in length. The only significant difference between these two types of ceratopian is in the detailed structure of the frill. While the frill of *Centrosaurus* is studded with small epoccipital bones, that of *Styracosaurus* has long pointed ones which look more like the brow or nose horns of *Triceratops*. Although it is far from certain at the moment, it is tempting to suggest that we may be looking at male and female of the same species. Perhaps the male dinosaur is the one with the decorative frill?

Other short frills include *Brachyrhinoceratops, Pachyrhinosaurus* and *Monoclonius.*

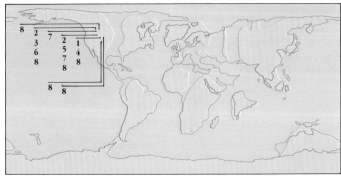

Map (above)

1 *Agathaumas* 5 *Monoclinius*
2 *Brachyceratops* 6 *Pachyrhinosaurus*
3 *Centrosaurus* 7 *Styracosaurus*
4 *Diceratops* 8 *Triceratops*

Above: Centrosaurus skeleton
The shoulder and neck region of this quadruped are strengthened to help bear the weight of the massive head.

Epoccipital bones

Left: *Styracosaurus skull*
This is distinguished by its frill in which the epoccipital bones have been drawn out into long spikes. These may have been used to attract mates.

Below: *Triceratops skull*
This had a short, solid frill encircled by a series of epoccipital bones giving the frill its wavy edge.

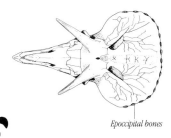

Epoccipital bones

Left: These **Ceratopid** footprints each measure 500mm (20 inches).

CERATOPIDS II

'Long-frilled' ceratopians have extraordinarily large heads, which are dominated by the long bony frill. As was the case with *Styracosaurus*, on the previous page, the frill may be decorated by a variety of bumps and small horns. By contrast, the remainder of the skeleton is virtually identical to that of the 'short-frilled' ceratopids.

The general body proportions of these animals are very reminiscent of living rhinoceroses: both are powerful, heavily built, four-footed animals with horns, and it is expected that they would have had rather similar life-styles.

Ceratopids were undoubtedly browsing herbivores. All have large heads and powerful jaws, lined with a battery of teeth. The teeth form scissor-like blades, which would have cut the vegeta-tion into short lengths (aided by enormously powerful jaw muscles), prior to being pulverised in the stomach. It is not certain whether all ceratopids had stomach stones, as did psittacosaurs, but it is possible that they had similar food grinding devices in the gut.

Torosaurus (bull reptile), in the foreground below, comes from Wyoming and its total length was almost 8 metres (26 ft), of which over 2.5 metres (8 ft) was head. This is the largest head known of any land living animal. The brow horns are very long and pointed, while the nose horn is quite small; however it is the frill which dominates the head. The frill is long and virtually unornamented, having a very smooth margin; it is also held at a low angle to the back of the head, so that it lies across the shoulders forming what appears to be a very effective defensive shield. However, while it may have had some purpose as a shield, it was undoubtedly mainly used for display between rival animals: the chin being lowered and the head being swung from side to side to give maximum display to the frill. It is possible that the frill was vividly coloured, in order to increase the visual effect of the display. Unfortu-

Pronunciation:	Ser-ah-tope-ids
Includes:	Pentaceratops, Arrhinoceratops, Chasmosaurus, Anchiceratops, Torosaurus, Eoceratops
Period:	Latest Cretaceous (80-64 mya)
Location:	Western North America

Below: *Pentaceratops*
As the name suggests, this was supposed to have five horns on its skull. The additional horns are in fact pointed cheek bones which are found in nearly all ceratopians.

Below: *Chasmosaurus*
Here the bony frill at the back of the skull is longer than the skull itself. The frill had large openings in its bony skeleton which were probably filled with muscle and covered with skin. The frill's edges were lined with small pointed bones.

Right: *Torosaurus*
The largest of the long-frilled ceratopians. One specimen has a skull 2.6m (8.5ft) long (the size of a small car) – the biggest head of any known land animal.

Above centre: *Anchiceratops*
*Similar to **Chasmosaurus**, except this had longer horns above the eyes and the frill was different, with smaller openings and three pairs of bony projections.*

nately traces of skin pigment are not preserved, even when skin impressions are, so we can never be sure of this.

Chasmosaurus (chasm reptile) from Alberta was a little smaller than *Torosaurus*, reaching a total body length of something like 5 metres (17 ft). Several fine skeletons of this ceratopian have been recovered. The skull is a little smaller than that of *Torosaurus*, but the frill is impressive and ornamented by a number of smaller epoccipitals around the margin. The brow horns also tend to be a little smaller than those of other long-frilled ceratopians.

Anchiceratops (close-horned face) again comes from the Red Deer River of Alberta. It differs from *Chasmosaurus* in that it has longer brow horns, and a pair of epoccipitals on the front near the top of the frill.

Pentaceratops (five-horned

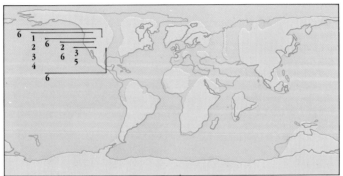

face) comes from New Mexico and appears to have reached lengths of about 7 metres (23 ft). The name is a little misleading, because it suggests that this ceratopian has more horns than usual. This is in fact a mistake! It was once thought that the large, pointed bones which stick out from the bottom edge of the skull (beneath the eye socket, and just in front of the bottom edge of the frill, labelled 'false horn' in the diagram) were real horns like the ones above the eye and on the nose. As careful examination will show, all ceratopians have this pointed bone at the back of the cheek (even protoceratopids, page 44); it is a normal part of the shape of the skull.

Window opening

Above: *Anchiceratops skull*
This form has a distinctive frill structure with small window openings and long, pointed eyebrow horns.

Right: *Chasmosaurus skeleton*
This skeleton is typical of a large, lumbering dinosaur. The hip and shoulder girdles, as well as the legs, are solidly built — designed for weight-bearing, not speed. Note the small blunt brow bones.

Below: *Comparative sizes*
1 Chasmosaurus: 5.2m (17ft)
2 Anchiceratops: 6m (20ft)
3 Pentaceratops: 7m (23ft)
4 Torosaurus: 7.6m (25ft)

Map (above)
1 Anchiceratops
2 Arrhinoceratops
3 Chasmosaurus
4 Eoceratops
5 Pentaceratops
6 Torosaurus

Right: *Pentaceratops skull*
As in all the long frilled forms, Pentaceratops has a long, low face and a tapering muzzle. Here you can see that the so-called cheek horns are really elongated bones, as in other species.

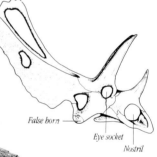

False horn

Eye socket

Nostril

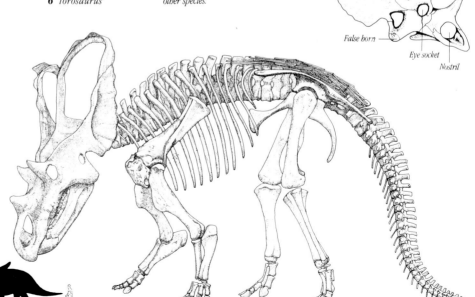

PACHYCEPHALOSAURS

The name pachycephalosaur means literally 'thick headed reptile'. Pachycephalosaurs belong to a group of rare and quite bizarre looking ornithischians, which like the preceding group (ceratopids) first appeared towards the end of the Cretaceous period. They have quite a long history in dinosaur studies, but have been shrouded in a lot of confusion because the early discoveries were very fragmentary bits and pieces. The first remains were discovered in the middle of the 19th century and comprised unusual teeth (which were given the name *Troodon* – 'wounding tooth') because of their sharp edges. At the turn of the century more teeth were found as well as a few broken pieces of the head-dome. The thick head bones were named *Stegoceras* ('horned roof') and thought to belong to a ceratopid, later they were thought

Pronunciation:	Pack-ee-sef-al-oh-sores
Includes:	Prenocephale, Pachycephalosaurus, Homalocephale, Stegoceras, Yaverlandia (southern England), Majungatholus (Malagasy)
Period:	Late Cretaceous (100-64 mya)
Location:	Mainly North America and Asia

Right: *Pachycephalosaurus*
This dinosaur had a massively thickened skull roof giving its head a domed appearance. The skull bones themselves became extremely thick and the effect is enhanced by extra bone nodules around the skull.

to belong to a stegosaur (page 52), until finally part of a skeleton and head were discovered near Edmonton in Alberta. The animal was called 'Troodon' after the first teeth, even though the head proved that it was similar to *Stegoceras*. As we see below, the animal is now called *Stegoceras*, and *Troodon* is thought to be a small carnivorous dinosaur rather like the coelurosaurs (page 12) in general shape. It could be that the early teeth found with the skull bones represent an association of predator (or scavenger) and the prey together – but this is very difficult to prove now.

Pachycephalosaurs have now been found quite extensively in eastern Asia (primarily Mongolia and northern China) as a result of several joint expeditions by Polish and Chinese scientists in the past 20 years. By contrast to discoveries elsewhere, some of these have been well preserved

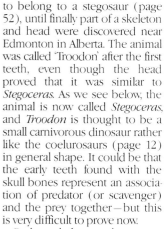

Below: *Stegoceras*
*Two types of adult **Stegoceras** can be distinguished: one group had thicker, heavier domes than the other. It is possible that these could be identified as males and females.*

Above: *Homalocephale*
This pachycephalosaur is unusual because parts of its skeleton are known in addition to its skull. Its wide hips suggest it gave birth to live young rather than laying eggs in typical dinosaur fashion.

Right: *Two pachycephalosaurs engage in the sort of violent head-butting contest for which their skulls made them unique. This established a social hierarchy within groups.*

and include parts of their skeletons. Dinosaur distributions in eastern Asia and western North America in the late Cretaceous are fairly common, but in recent years reports have come in of pachycephalosaurs in both Europe (one very fragmentary specimen from the early Cretaceous) and a well preserved partial skull from Malagasy (Madagascar).

The new discoveries in Mongolia have revealed a number of features that are unexpected in the group. One of the most important is related to the hip bones; these look more like those of ankylosaurids (page 58) than ornithopods and have been used to propose that pachycephalosaurs are a completely separate group of ornithishians (rather than just a bizarre group

Map (below)

1 *Goyocephale*
2 *Gravitholus*
3 *Homalcephale*
4 *Majungatholus*
5 *Micropachycephalosaurus*
6 *Ornatotholus*
7 *Pachycephalosaurus*
8 *Prenocephale*
9 *Stegoceras*
10 *Stygimoloch*
11 *Troödon*
12 *Tylocephale*
13 *Yaverlandia*

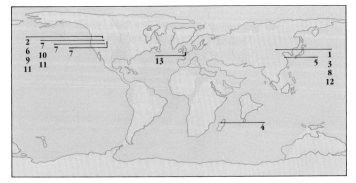

Below: *Stegoceras skeleton*
This skeleton is poorly known and this reconstruction is based on comparison with other ornithischians and some guesswork! Some parts of the skeleton have been interpreted as

adaptations to head-butting: the head is offset at an angle to the neck vertebrae and the back vertebrae are held tightly together by ossified tendons. Note the presence of ribs in the belly.

Above: *Teeth of Troödon*
The first Troödon specimens to be discovered were teeth. They belonged to a carnivore animal and would have been used to slice meat, but were at first associated with pachycephalosaurs.

Below: *Comparative sizes*
1 *Stegoceras: 2m (6.5ft)*
2 *Homalocephale: 3m (10ft)*
3 *Pachycephalosaurus: 8m (26ft)*

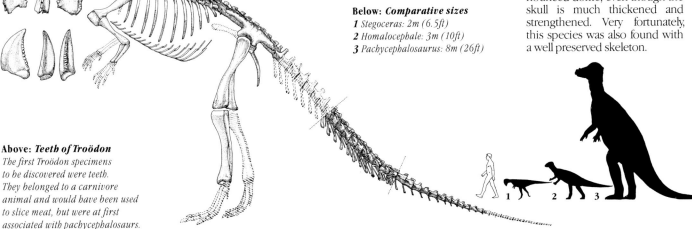

of ornithopods which are distant relatives of the hypsilophodontids). This idea is not totally accepted yet, but is one of the reasons for considering them in this separate section here.

Stegoceras is small by dinosaur standards 2 metres (6 ft) long, and in its body shape is most closely similar to ornithopods such as the hypsilophodontids (page 36). The backbone and tail of this dinosaur had very stiff joints; these helped it to withstand the force of head-butting, because the thickness of bone on the head was used to absorb the impact of head-to-head butting contests, rather like the horns of sheep, goats or deer.

Prenocephale (sloping head) is the Mongolian equivalent of *Stegoceras* in terms of general size and shape. It differs mainly in the arrangement of the small knobs and ridges around the sides of the skull, which were probably for individual recognition.

Pachycephalosaurus is the largest pachycephalosaur known, estimated at 8 metres (28 ft) long, unfortunately it is only known from one almost complete skull (plus a few fragmentary pieces of head-dome). The rest of the skeleton has never been recognised.

Homalocephale (even head) in another Mongolian form, unusual because it lacks a pronounced dome, even though the skull is much thickened and strengthened. Very fortunately, this species was also found with a well preserved skeleton.

STEGOSAURS

Stegosaurs are medium-sized, four-footed dinosaurs, which are particularly distinctive because they tend to have rows of either big bony plates or spines (or a combination of both). Very few stegosaurs have been found, but *Stegosaurus* (not to be confused with *Stegoceras* which is a pachycephalosaur — page 50) from Colorado, Wyoming and Utah (USA) is one of the best known of dinosaurs.

Almost all the remains of stegosaurs come from late Jurassic rocks and have been found in Europe, Africa, India and China as well as in North America. As has been so often the case, the earliest discoveries (in Britain in the early 1870s) went largely unrecognised because they were incomplete. But just a few years later, in the late 1870s, some fabulous remains were discovered at Como Bluff in Wyoming, including virtually complete skeletons. In recent years significant new discoveries have been made in the Jurassic rocks of south western China, which have added greatly to our knowledge of the range and variety of this type of dinosaur.

Pronunciation:	Steg-oh-sores
Includes:	Stegosaurus, Kentrosaurus, Tuojiangosaurus
Period:	Late Jurassic (with a straggler into the late Cretaceous) (170-70 mya)
Location:	North America, Asia, Europe, Africa, India

Below: *Tuojiangosaurus*
This is the best preserved of the known stegosaurids from China. It is seen in a typically stegosaurid pose, using its low slung head to browse on plants. The plates running along its body are conical in shape.

Right: *Kentrosaurus*
The spikes here are distinctive. Those near the front of the body are flat and plate-like. Along the back and tail are narrow spines with a pair of spines pointing backwards from the pelvis.

Above: *Comparative sizes*
1 Stegosaurus: 6-7.5m (20-24ft)
2 Tuojiangosaurus: 6m (20ft)
3 Kentrosaurus: 2.5m (8.2ft)

Above: *Stegosaurus*
Although several skeletons have been found, there is confusion as to whether the plates along the back stood upright or lay flat.

Stegosaurus (roofed reptile), which gave its name to the group as a whole, is one of the largest of known stegosaurs, but is still only modestly sized compared with other dinosaurs. The largest species reached a length of about 8 metres (25 ft) and probably weighed about 1.5 tonnes.

Stegosaurus shows a range of unusual body features. Firstly the front legs are only about one half of the length of the back legs, so that when walking the body slopes strongly forward and downward toward the ground. This brings and keeps the head very close to the ground, which probably indicates that stegosaurs fed on ground cover plants. How-ever, having said this, it has been suggested that stegosaurs (and *Stegosaurus* in particular) may have been able to rear up onto their hind legs, using the tail as a counterbalance, to feed on higher foliage; there is certainly nothing in the skeleton to prevent them from adopting this sort of posture for short periods of time.

Another famous feature of *Stegosaurus* is the size and shape of its head. The head is long and thin, and was probably adapted for feeding on certain types of vegetation (though what this was we are not yet certain); also the part of the head surrounding the brain is very small, as was the brain itself. This has given rise to the idea that dinosaurs had very small brains, and were by implication rather stupid creatures. In fact *Stegosaurus* had an adequate brain for its needs, and was not particularly unintelligent — and other dinosaurs had very large, bird-like brains and were clearly 'smart' creatures by any standards.

The dominant feature of all stegosaurs is their bony armour plating. Their main means of defence would have been the tail. In all stegosaurs the tail is equipped with large, pointed spikes which could have been swished from side to side, by powerful tail muscles, to inflict fearful wounds upon predators.

The larger plates ranged down the back were not defensive, but seem to have acted as heat controllers. The plates were made of spongy bone and were blood-filled and could be used either as radiators to lose heat to the air when the animal was hot, or as solar panels to warm the body.

Kentrosaurus comes from Tanzania. It is considerably smaller and more 'prickly' than *Stegosaurus*, lacking many of the large control plates seen in the latter species, but this fits well with the animal's smaller size.

Tuojiangosaurus from the late Jurassic of China is intermediate in size and in the shape of its back plates.

Map (right)

1	Chialingosaurus	6	Kentrosaurus
2	Craterosaurus	7	Lexovisaurus
3	Dacentrurus	8	Paranthodon
4	Dravidosaurus	9	Stegosaurus
5	Huayangosaurus	10	Tuojiangosaurus
		11	Wuerhosaurus

Below: *Stegosaurus skull and teeth*
This skull seems rather small and the jaw rather weak for such a large animal. The teeth are numerous, leaf-shaped and serrated, but are not organised into a grinding battery.

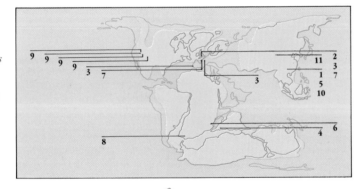

Above: *It has been suggested that **Stegosaurus'** back plates acted as armour plating, protecting these slow moving creatures from predators. However, this is improbable as the drawing shows that the flanks and belly would still have been vulnerable to attack.*

Left: *Stegosaurus skeleton*
This skeleton shows the features very well: the relatively small head, the short front legs compared to the back ones, and the large bony plates along the back. The tail spikes were used for defence, swung from side to side by powerful tail muscles.

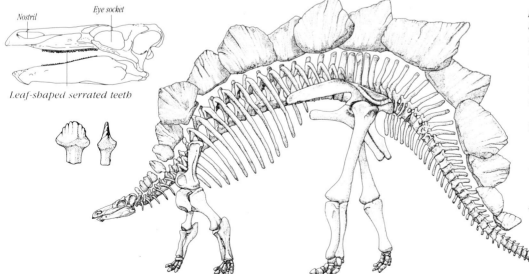

Nostril

Eye socket

Leaf-shaped serrated teeth

SCELIDOSAURUS

Pronunciation:	Skel-ide-oh-sore-us
Includes:	Scelidosaurus, possibly Lusitanosaurus
Period:	Early Jurassic
	(185 mya)
Location:	Western Europe, possibly south western USA

Below: *Scelidosaurus*

This restoration is based upon illustrations prepared for the British Museum of Natural History. The back is studded with rows of low conical bones and just behind the head these are modified into peculiar tricorn arrays, possibly for extra protection. The long tail may have counterbalanced the front end of the body.

In the late 1850s an almost complete dinosaur skeleton was recovered from the cliffs on the coast at Lyme Regis (Dorset, England). The rocks in this part of Britain were laid down on the bottom of the sea in early Jurassic times, and most fossils found here are of large marine reptiles (ichthyosaurs and plesiosaurs). Land animals such as dinosaurs are very rare finds in these locations because their remains would have had to have been washed out to sea before burial, so the discovery of *Scelidosaurus* was very lucky indeed. Since the time of the first discovery, scelidosaur remains have been found only rarely. Earlier this century a small nodule was found on the sea shore, which contained much of the skeleton of a tiny *Scelidosaurus*, and recent fragmentary remains include parts of the skull and impressions of the skin.

The largest skeleton of *Scelidosaurus* (the one discovered in the 1850s) is of an animal of about 4 metres (13 ft) in length. It is not certain whether this is the maximum size that this dinosaur could attain, but these are the largest bones known to date. The large skeleton (and the small one in the nodule) have been almost completely prepared out of the rock in which they were discovered by the highly skilled preparators in the laboratories in the British Museum (Natural History). It is therefore likely that we shall know a great deal more about this animal in the near future.

What we know to date is that *Scelidosaurus* is quite a heavily built dinosaur, with strong pillar-

like back legs and broad four-toed feet. The front legs were until recently completely unknown, because they are missing from the large skeleton as well as the small one. However, some new material recently discovered appears to show that the upper arm was a broad, stout bone which fits well with the idea that this dinosaur walked on all four legs, rather than just the hind ones. The skin of the back and flanks was studded with small conical plates, which seem similar to the armour plating seen in the skin of ankylosaurids and nodosaurids (pages 56-59). Just behind the head, and on either side, the stud-like armour is arranged into two clusters of three.

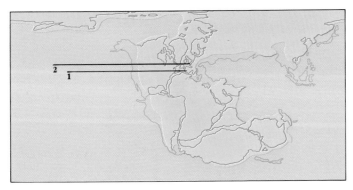

Map (left)
1 *Lusitanosaurus*
2 *Scelidosaurus*

The head of *Scelidosaurus* is rather deeper and squatter than those of stegosaurids (page 52) and seems more like that of ankylosaurs. However, there is no great degree of development of extra bony plates welded onto the sides and top for added protection. There is a large plate of bone welded to the side of the lower jaw and evidence of extra bone welded to the head bones.

The teeth are simple and leaf-shaped and extend right down to the tip of the upper jaw, which would have made the horny beak extremely small, rather like the situation in the *Lesothosaurus*.

Scelidosaurus would have been a slow moving plant eater, which relied on its armoured skin to protect it from the large predators of the time. It was very much like a larger and more cumbersome relative of *Scutellosaurus* (page 34). Very recently it has been suggested that more *Scelidosaurus*-like material has been found in early Jurassic rocks from south western USA.

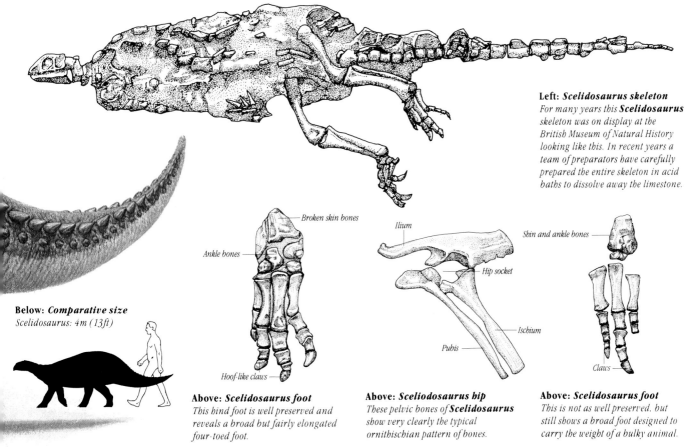

Left: *Scelidosaurus skeleton*
*For many years this **Scelidosaurus** skeleton was on display at the British Museum of Natural History looking like this. In recent years a team of preparators have carefully prepared the entire skeleton in acid baths to dissolve away the limestone.*

Below: *Comparative size*
Scelidosaurus: 4m (13ft)

Broken skin bones

Ankle bones

Hoof-like claws

Ilium

Hip socket

Ischium

Pubis

Shin and ankle bones

Claws

Above: *Scelidosaurus foot*
This hind foot is well preserved and reveals a broad but fairly elongated four-toed foot.

Above: *Sceliodosaurus hip*
*These pelvic bones of **Scelidosaurus** show very clearly the typical ornithischian pattern of bones.*

Above: *Scelidosaurus foot*
This is not as well preserved, but still shows a broad foot designed to carry the weight of a bulky animal.

NODOSAURIDS

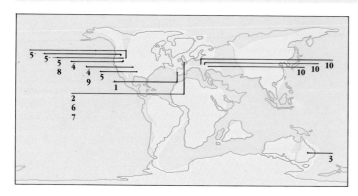

Pronunciation:	No-doh-sore-ids
Includes:	Nodosaurus, Hylaeosaurus, Polacanthus
Period:	Late Jurassic to late Cretaceous (145-70 mya)
Location:	North America, Europe, possibly Australia

Map (above)

1 *Dracopelta*	**6** *Polacanthus*
2 *Hylaeosaurus*	**7** *Sarcolestes*
3 *Minmi*	**8** *Sauropelta*
4 *Nodosaurus*	**9** *Silvisaurus*
5 *Panoplosaurus*	**10** *Struthiosaurus*

Below: *Nodosaurus*

The armour is the most distinctive feature of this dinosaur. It consisted of broad bands of alternatively large and small rounded nodules (hence its name).

The last major group of dinosaurs that we will be looking at are the truly armoured ones and are known by the general name of ankylosaurs (fused, or welded together, reptiles). The name comes from the fact that the bony plates in the skin of these animals are often welded together to form a shell-like armour — particularly over the skull. Ankylosaurs are known from rocks which date from the late part of the Jurassic, when they are a rather rare species in dinosaur communities, until the late Cretaceous, when they become quite abundant. Ankylosaurs have been divided into two groups or families: the nodosaurids and the ankylosaurids. They all share a number of features, such as being medium-sized, the largest being about 7 metres long (27 ft), but extremely heavily built, with four

Below: *Hylaeosaurus*

This dinosaur is frustratingly incomplete as the skeleton is embedded in a block of limestone in the British Museum. The arrangement of its armour is speculative.

Below: *Polacanthus*

This reconstruction is also largely guesswork. The long spines may have formed a protective frill around the sides of the body to guard the flanks and the neck from attack.

Below: *Comparative sizes*
1 *Hylaeosaurus: 4m (13ft)*
2 *Polacanthus: 4m (13ft)*
3 *Nodosaurus: 5.5m (18ft)*

short, strong, pillar-like legs. Their heads tend to be low, broad and heavily armoured. The armour on the backs and flanks of these animals can vary quite a lot in detail, and in some cases the tail can have a large bony club on its end. The nodosaurids are discussed on these pages, followed by the ankylosaurids.

Hylaeosaurus was the first nodosaurid dinosaur discovered and was close to being one of the first dinosaurs ever to be found. It was named *Hylaeosaurus* (woodland or forest reptile) by Gideon Mantell, who discovered its remains in a quarry near Cuckfield in the county of Sussex, England in 1833. The remains come from rocks which date from the early Cretaceous period. The fossilised remains of

Hylaeosaurus comprise the front half of a well preserved skeleton embedded in a large chunk of stone. It shows that the animal had rows of large curved spines arranged along the back, but unfortunately little else will be known until the specimen is prepared out of the rock. The reconstruction seen below is largely guesswork.

Polacanthus (many spikes) is another British nodosaurid dinosaur discovered in 1865 in early Cretaceous rocks on the southern coast of the Isle of Wight (a small island just off the southern coast of Britain). The skeleton consisted of a large part of the hind end of the dinosaur, the remainder having probably been lost a little earlier in a cliff fall. Frustratingly, even though this dinosaur lived at about the same time

as *Hylaeosaurus*, and in the same part of the world, their skeletons do not overlap. It is therefore impossible to compare them and prove whether — as some suspect — that these two are really one and the same dinosaur.

Nodosaurus (lumpy reptile) comes from the late Cretaceous of Kansas and Wyoming, USA. It appears that the whole of its upper surface was covered in a mat of closely fitting plates of bone. The band of larger and smaller bones would have provided not only great strength to

deter the teeth and claws of predators, but also allows some flexibility; a similar feature is seen on the back of species of armadillo, where the shell is divided into bands so that these creatures can roll into a ball—not that *Nodosaurus* could ever have rolled into a ball!

In addition to the heavy armouring, the skulls are unusual because they show that these dinosaurs had a separate air passage from the nose to the back of the throat — a feature that is not normally found in reptiles.

Below: *The massive construction of the nodosaurid skull is plainly seen in this photograph of **Panoplosaurus**, a late Cretaceous dinosaur from North America. Large slabs of bone are plastered all over the skull. The skull is narrow with a pointed snout. Although the jaws are huge, they are not specially modified for grinding. The front of both the upper and lower jaws ends in a toothless, horn-covered beak.*

Above: *Polacanthus skeleton*
Though lacking a head and much of the front part of the body, the spikes and rear part are well preserved. The hips were covered by a mosaic of small bony nodules.

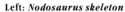

Left: *Pair of **Nodosaurid** footprints, each measuring 400mm (16 inches) in length.*

Left: *Nodosaurus skeleton*
It is a sad fact that nodosaurids are poorly known at present. This reconstruction has been given extra material from other nodosaurids, as the specimen was badly preserved. The armour plating is distinctive, consisting of bands of rounded nodules. It is not known whether this animal had a fringe of longer spikes as other nodosaurids did.

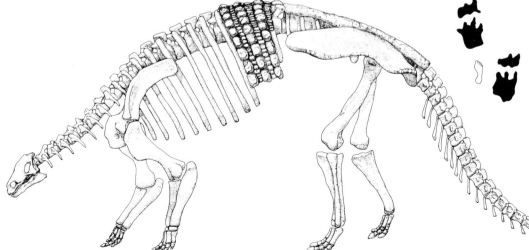

ANKYLOSAURIDS

Ankylosaurids, the second family of ankylosaurs, can be distinguished from nodosaurids quite easily. Ankylosaurids tend to have shorter and broader heads, with large triangular horns at the rear corners of the skull. Also the body armour tends not to have too many tall curved spines, but, most important of all, the tail ends in a massive, heavy bony club. Ankylosaurids seem to be restricted to the last half of the Cretaceous period, and are only so far found in western North America and eastern Asia. Ankylosaurid armour is found quite frequently, which suggests that they were fairly abundant animals at this time, but frustratingly few good skeletons have been discovered. *Euoplocephalus* (true plated head) is one of the best known

of this type of dinosaur, and we will confine ourselves to considering this one as a representative of them all.

Euoplocephalus was first discovered in 1902 near the Red Deer River, Alberta, Canada and over the years, as more material has been amassed, it has been possible to piece together a picture of the whole animal (see below). As was the case with nodosaurids, the legs are short and extremely powerful. The evident enormous weight of the armour plating of the skeleton and the relative shortness of the legs suggested to early palaeontologists that these dinosaurs (and nodosaurids as well) must have had a squat posture, shuffling along with their bellies touching the ground and the legs held out sideways from the

Pronunciation:	An-kile-oh-sore-ids
Includes:	Euoplocephalus, Pinacosaurus
Period:	Late Cretaceous (100-64 mya)
Location:	Western North America, eastern Asia

Below: *Euoplocephalus*
One of the largest ankylosaurs, its back was armoured with heavy nodules of bone set into leathery skin. Its tail club was a formidable weapon.

Right: *Pinacosaurus*
This dinosaur was of slender build. Its back and tail were covered with bony spines and the end of its tail bore a heavy bony club.

shoulders and hips. Modern views do not agree with this idea; the arrangement of the bones in the shoulders and hips are such that the legs have to be held beneath the body. More conclusive still is the evidence from ankylosaur trackways which show that the footprints of left and right feet were close together rather than splayed widely apart.

Another curious feature is to be found in the back and tail. Bony tendons are found alongside the backbone, but not as densely as in ornithopod dinosaurs (page 40). However, they are also found in the tail, close to the club. It seems likely that the tendons here provided firm anchorage for the powerful tail pulling muscles, so that they could swing the club from side to side, and also so that the tail would be stiffened to prevent 'whip lash' from damaging the tail bones when the club

smashed against the body of one of its attackers.

Ankylosaurids were seemingly very well adapted to survive life in the late Cretaceous. This was the time of the giant tyrannosaurids (page 24) the largest and most powerful dinosaur predators that had ever appeared, and yet the ankylosaurids seem to have found the perfect solution to the danger of such predators. Firstly, their armour was virtually impregnable to the teeth and claws of tyrannosaurs, but more important even than that was the danger that they posed to tyrannosaurs. Tyrannosaurs may have had one fatal weakness as far as ankylosaurs were concerned – the risk of falling over! A well aimed swipe with a tail club could have toppled the largest tyrannosaur, with the risk of breaking a leg, which would have proved fatal for such a huge animal.

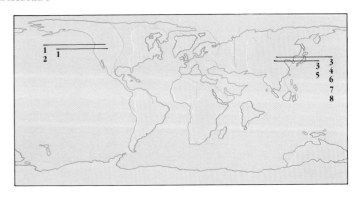

Map (above)
1 *Ankylosaurus*   5 *Sauroplites*
2 *Euoplocephalus*   6 *Shamosaurus*
3 *Pinacosaurus*   7 *Talarurus*
4 *Saichania*   8 *Tarchia*

Below: *Comparative sizes*
1 *Pinacosaurus: 5m (16ft)*
2 *Euoplocephalus: 6m (20ft)*

Below: *Euoplocephalus skeleton*
Here the enormous size of the tail club can be seen in comparison to the rest of the body. Several bones embedded in the skin at the end of

the tail were greatly enlarged. They became fused to one another and to the last few tail bones to form this heavy club. It could be swung from side to side by strong tail muscles.

Below: *Self defence*
Here **Euoplocephalus** is shown swinging its heavy tail club against the tyrannosaurid in order to topple and so disable the predator.

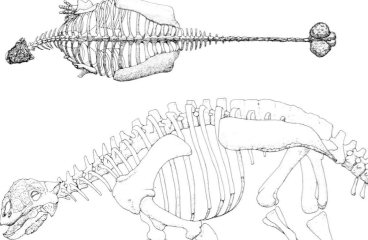

Left: *Euoplocephalus skeleton*
In this ankylosaurid skeleton you can see the characteristic armoured head with its toothless beak, the shortish neck and the strongly built legs.

The legs are tucked in, underneath the body. The vertebral spines in the hip region are welded together, giving a larger attachment area for hip muscles.

THE EXTINCTION OF DINOSAURS

The extinction of dinosaurs is a very popular subject, with no end of theories to explain the sudden disappearance of all dinosaurs at the end of the Cretaceous period, 64 million years ago. Most theories fail to convince the experts because it was not only the dinosaurs that became extinct, but a whole variety of animals including ammonites, plesiosaurs, ichythyosaurs and chalky plankton in the sea, pterosaurs in the air, dinosaurs and many other large creatures on land. This is known as a mass extinction. On the other hand, crocodiles did not all become extinct, nor did bony fish or most plant species, mammals or birds. Finding a cause which will explain the selective nature of the extinctions is very difficult.

At the present time, there seem to be two main areas of research into this subject. The first and most popular theory at the moment is a cosmic one.

Left: *This photograph shows the explorers who discovered the Hoba West meteorite in Africa in 1920. The largest meteorite discovered, this would have been dwarfed by the one supposed to have caused the end of dinosaurs.*

Below: *Comet Ikeya-Seki, vivid in the night sky. One theory favours comet showers resulting from disturbances in the Oort Cloud (a field of comets orbiting the sun) as the cause of periodic extinctions.*

The Cosmic Theory

Some years ago, the discovery in Italy and Denmark of a layer of clay, at the end of a Cretaceous sequence of rocks, containing unexpectedly high levels of iridium provoked the meteorite extinction theory. Iridium is a heavy metal which is not normally found in large amounts in the earth's crust. One potential source of iridium, however, is extra-terrestrial: from meteorites, asteroids and comets. This theory suggests that a large meteorite 10-15 kilometres (6-9 miles) wide may have crashed into the earth causing a massive explosion on impact. This would have caused enormous dust and water clouds which would have shrouded the earth for a long period of time – possibly several weeks or months, or even longer.

This shroud of dust and water vapour would have cut out the light from the sun which is essential for plant growth and would have caused extreme cold. This would result in the extinction of many groups. The animals best able to survive may well have been the smaller opportunistic ones who scavenged for food (eg mammals, lizards, crocodiles and snakes), rather than the larger, more specialised creatures.

This theory has become very popular in recent years because of the increasing awareness of what the environmental effects may be of a nuclear war on this planet. It is quite possible that a nuclear war would have a similar affect upon the atmosphere (not to mention the radio-active fall-out) to a meteorite impact, as implicated in the extinction of dinosaurs.

Climatic Change Theory

The other theory depends upon the cumulative effect of continental movement, through tectonic activity (see Introduction, page 6). Movement of continents (such as the ones seen during the time of the dinosaurs) across climatic belts may have caused severe changes in climatic conditions. Evidence to support this theory comes from careful geological analysis of North America, showing that the general climate worsened towards the end of the Cretaceous period, causing a marked but gradual change in plant and animal species. During the last 10 million years of the Cretaceous period, the world became increasingly seasonal, rather than pleasantly warm all year round.

It seems at least possible that a deterioration of climatic conditions may have caused widespread changes in the ecology of the globe. The result of this would have been a major change in the floras and faunas of the time, and an inevitable change in the types of animals and plants best suited to these new conditions. About 5 to 10 million years from the end of the Cretaceous period this planet's vegetation was very lush with many tropical and sub-tropical species of plants—

ideal conditions to support a rich and varied dinosaur fauna. However, towards the end of this period the flora changed dramatically to one dominated by cool, temperate woodland plants, resulting in the decline of the dinosaurs. It is possible that dinosaurs and some of the other groups that became extinct in the sea, in the air and on the land were well suited to life in the Mesozoic, but not in the harsher conditions of the following Tertiary Period.

In both of these theories, the survivors are presumed to be the most rugged sorts of organism and the best able to survive changes in their environment. Unfortunately the dinosaurs were unable to survive the test.

GEOGRAPHY OF DINOSAUR FINDS

This map gives some impression of how widespread dinosaur discoveries are, with all continents, including Antarctica, producing dinosaur remains.

North America

The first important discoveries in the 1850s were in western and eastern North America, followed by dramatic finds in Wyoming and Colorado. North America has been an extremely rich hunting ground for dinosaurs, with discoveries from all three periods of the Mesozoic right across the continent. Remains of dinosaurs have been found in Alberta, Arizona, Connecticut, Montana, New England, New Mexico, South Dakota and Utah. The most recent discoveries have been in the far north of Alaska.

South America

Dinosaurs were first discovered in South America in the late 1900s. Most finds have been made in southern Brazil and Argentina where Mesozoic rocks are quite widespread. Careful excavation work in recent years has resulted in important, well-preserved remains.

Europe

Western Europe has a long history of dinosaur discoveries. The Triassic, Jurassic and Cretaceous rocks in Germany have all yielded dinosaur remains, including the famous *Plateosaurus* quarries of Halberstadt and Trössingen. Discoveries have been made in the Jurassic rocks of central western Britain and many *Iguanodon* skeletons have been found in the Cretaceous rocks of southern England, Belgium, Germany and Spain. Some well-preserved remains are also known from Romania and southern France.

Central Asia

Expeditions to Mongolia in the early years of this century revealed rich dinosaur-bearing rocks. Interesting finds have also been made in the Gobi Desert.

China

China has extensive Triassic, Jurassic and Cretaceous rocks that have begun to yield large numbers of dinosaurs in recent years, particularly in north eastern China and the Sichuan Province.

Australia and India

To date, most Australian dinosaur finds have been rather poor, but it is probably only a matter of time before rich dinosaur-bearing localities are found. The Kota area of central India has abundant remains of *Barapasaurus*, and stegosaur remains have been discovered in southern India.

Africa

Triassic and early Jurassic rocks in southern Africa have yielded prosauropod and ornithopod remains. Dinosaurs have also been discovered in Tanzania, the central Sahara, Morocco and Niger.

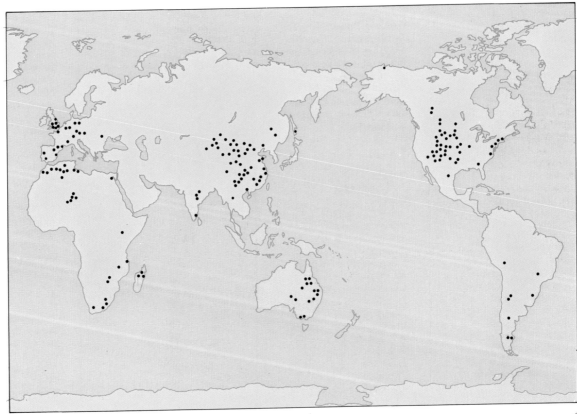

Right: *This world map shows many of the important localities where dinosaur discoveries have been made. It is at once obvious how widespread was the dispersal of the dinosaurs on land. New expeditions will no doubt extend the picture even further. In fact, the latest major discovery has been made in Antarctica where a new dinosaur has recently been collected. It was found in late Cretaceous rocks and appears to be a hypsilophodontid. A map of dinosaur discoveries made in the middle of the last century would have looked very different because, at that time, remains were only known from Europe (England and Germany) and from North America.*

GLOSSARY

A

Absolute dating
A means of estimating the age of rocks with some degree of accuracy using measurements of radioactive isotopes.

Algae
Aquatic plants, both small and large.

Ammonites
Extinct coiled shellfish that were abundant in Mesozoic seas, relatives of squid, octopus and *Nautilus* today.

Amphibious
Able to live both in water and on land.

Archosaurs
A major group of reptiles including the dinosaurs, pterosaurs, thecodontians — all of which are extinct — and the living crocodiles.

Arthropods
Animals with jointed legs, e.g. insects, spiders, crabs and shrimps.

Articulated
Jointed together or jointed.

Asiamerica
The land areas of Asia and America joined by a land bridge formed by the Bering Straits during the Mesozoic Era.

B

Biped
An habitually two-footed creature.

Brachiopods
Shelled sea creatures that look a little like clams and oysters but are not closely related.

Browsers
Those animals that feed on high foliage (shrubs and trees).

C

Cambrian Period
The most ancient of the Palaeozoic time zones, rocks from this period show the first traces of fairly complicated animal life.

Cantilever
A beam or lever that projects outward from its support (e.g. the tail of a dinosaur projects from the pelvis as a cantilever and so balances the front part of the body).

Chevrons
Bones hanging below the tail.

Clavicle
Collar bone.

Community
The local environment of an organism.

Comparative dating
A technique for estimating the age of rocks based on their characteristic fossils; these can be compared with those from rocks elsewhere, as similarly aged rocks are expected to have similar fossil species.

Conifers
Cone-bearing trees such as firs, pines and yews.

Conservation
The procedure used to ensure that a fossil once excavated does not deteriorate.

Continental Drift
The phenomenon of continental movement (Drift) on tectonic plates in the Earth's crust.

Cranial
Relating to the cranium or braincase.

Cretaceous Period
The third period in the Mesozoic Era. It lasted from 135 million years ago until the extinction of the dinosaurs about 64 million years ago.

Cycads
Squat, rather palm-tree-like plants that were particularly abundant in the Mesozoic Era.

D

Decay
To rot, to distintegrate.

Dentition
Teeth.

Deposit (geological)
Accumulation of rock.

Dinosaur
A special type of land-living reptile with an erect gait — a member of the archosaur group — that flourished between 225 and 64 million years ago. Dinosaurs can be classified in two orders: Saurischia and Ornithischia. The term is from the Greek, meaning, 'terrible, or fearfully great reptile'.

'Dinosauroid'
Dale Russell's name for his imaginative reconstruction of how the theropod dinosaur *Stenonychosaurus* might have looked if it had not gone extinct 64 million years ago.

E

Ecology
The study of the relationship between organisms and the environment.

Embryo
An animal in its earliest stages of development.

Epoccipital
Small bone edging the frill on the skulls of ceratopian dinosaurs.

Erosion
The result of weathering on exposed rocks.

Euramerica
The land areas of Europe and America which were joined for much of the Mesozoic Era.

Eurasia
The land areas of Europe and Asia joined as they are today.

Evolution
A gradual change in the characteristics of a population of organisms over a series of generations brought about through natural selection.

Extinction
The death of a species.

F

Family
A grouping of similar genera.

Fauna
Animals.

Femur
Upper leg or thigh-bone.

Fenestra
Window-like opening in skull.

Fibula
Shin bone (see also **tibia**).

Flora
Plants.

Foliage
Leaves, branches and twigs.

Foreclimbs
Front legs or arms/wings.

Fossil
A fossil is the preserved remains of something that once lived. It can be formed in a number of way, usually involving burial and chemical change.

Fossilisation
The process that leads to the formation of fossils.

Fused
Joined, welded together very firmly.

G

Gait
Characteristics of movement.

Geographical distribution
The localities where an animal or plant may be found.

Geological timescale
A timescale of the history of the Earth arrived at by a combination of comparative and absolute dating of rocks and their fossils worldwide.

Geologist
A person who studies rocks.

Geology
The science of the study of rocks.

Ginkgo
The maidenhair tree of East Asia; the sole survivor of a once abundant group of gymnosperm trees.

Gondwana
The 'southern continents' in the Triassic Period, comprising South America, Africa, India, Antarctica and Australia.

Grazers
Those animals that feed on grasses (and other low-lying vegetation).

H

Hadrosaurine
Non-crested hadrosaurid.

Hindlimbs
Back or rear legs.

Humerus
Upper arm bone.

I

Ichthyosaurs
Marine reptiles of the Mesozoic Era; these were the most highly specialised of swimming reptiles with streamlined, fish-shaped bodies.

Ilium
One of the bones of the pelvis; it is

connected to the vertebral column (backbone).

Iridium
A heavy metal element found in meteorites and the Earth's core.

Ischium
One of the pelvic bones; it points downward and backward from the hip socket.

J

Jurassic Period
The second period in the Mesozoic Era; it lasted from 200-135 million years ago.

L

Lambeosaurine
Relating to hadrosaurids with large tubular crests on skull.

Laurasia
The 'northern continents' in the Triassic Period, comprising North America, Europe and Asia. Separated from Gondwana by Tethys.

Ligaments
Tough sheets or threads of protein (collagen) which support joints between bones.

M

Mass-extinction
The simultaneous extinction of a whole range of species.

Mesozoic
'Middle life'; the period of time (Era) between 225-64 million years ago when the dinosaurs reigned supreme — incorporates the Triassic, Jurassic and Cretaceous Periods.

Metacarpals
Long bones in the upper part of the hand that form the palm.

Metatarsals
Long bones in the upper part of the foot.

O

Omnivore
An animal with a diet of both plant and animal food.

Order
A category of animals that includes a variety of similar families.

Ornithischian
One of the two major Orders of dinosaurs (see also **saurischian**) which is based on hip structure. In ornithischians the pubis lies parallel to the ischium (as in birds). The group is entirely herbivorous and includes ornithopods, stegosaurs, ceratopians, ankylosaurs and pachycephalosaurs.

P

Palaeontologist
A person who studies fossils.

Palaeontology
The study of fossils.

Pangaea
The enormous supercontinent formed in late Permian times when all the continents of the Earth collided.

Pelvis
The hip region of the skeleton.

Petrification
'Turning to stone': the replacement, by minerals, of the original hard tissues of a fossilised organism, so that it eventually becomes stone-like in nature.

Plate tectonics
The study of the large plates which make up the Earth's crust, and their relative movements.

Plesiosaurs
Marine reptiles of the Mesozoic Era which swam using large flippers.

Posture
Normal standing or walking position of an animal.

Precambrian
Referring to the vast Period of time (before the Cambrian Period) that elapsed while the Earth cooled and became a solid planet which eventually developed its own climate and ecosystems with simple forms of life (4,500-600 million years ago).

Predatory
Preying upon other animals; referring to a hunting-and-killing style of life.

Pterosaurs
The flying reptiles of the Mesozoic Era; these are distant cousins of the dinosaurs.

Pubis
One of the pelvic bones, this usually points downward and forward from the hip socket. In some reptiles: ornithischian dinosaurs, segnosaurids and birds, the pubis lies parallel to the ischium.

Q

Quadruped
An habitually four-footed creature.

Quaternary Period
The recent prehistoric past dominated by the arrival of Man; 1.8 million years ago to the present day.

R

Radius
One of the two forearm bones (see also **ulna**).

S

Saurischian
One major grouping of the dinosaurs (based on hip structure) in which the pubis is long and points forward and downward from the hip socket; includes the carnivorous theropods and the herbivorous sauropodomorphs.

Sauropodomorphs
Large herbivorous saurischian dinosaurs including the prosauropods and sauropods.

Sedimentary rocks
Rocks that have formed from sediments, for example, sands and clays.

Serrated
With a notched edge like the cutting edge of a saw.

Silt
Grains, or finely broken pieces of rock that slowly settle out of water.

Stratum
A rock layer.

Stromatolites
Banded rocks that were made by blue-green algae; abundant in the Precambrian in particular.

Supercontinents
Extra large continents formed by the joining together of several continental areas i.e. Laurasia, Gondwana, Pangaea.

T

Talons
Sharp claws.

Tethys
A sea which in former times separated Laurasia from Gondwana. A remnant of this seaway is the Mediterranean.

Terrestrial
On or of the Earth's surface — land-dwelling.

Tertiary Period
This follows the Cretaceous Period and charts the rise of mammals from 64 million years ago up to the recent past (1.8 million years ago, the start of the Quaternary Period)

Theropods
A wide range of predatory saurischian dinosaurs, most of which were bipedal; commonly divided into two artificial groupings as 'coelurosaurs' (small theropods), and 'carnosaurs' (big theropods).

Tibia
The main shin bone (one of two, see also **fibula**).

Tooth battery
A large number of interlocking teeth arranged in a jaw to form a cutting or grinding surface.

Triassic Period
The first period of the Mesozoic Era; it lasted from 225-200 million years ago, and the dinosaurs first appeared towards its close.

U

Ulna
One of the two forearm bones (see also **radius**).

V

Variable gait
The ability to walk in a variety of ways depending upon how the legs are positioned.

Vertebra
An individual bone of the back (vertebral column=backbone).

Vertebrates
Animals with backbones e.g. fish, amphibians, reptiles, birds and mammals.

INDEX

Abrictosaurus, 34, *35*
Africa, 9, 10, 12, 22, 27, 30, 32, 34, 36, 38, 52, 61
Agathaumus, *47*
Albertosaurus, 24, *24*, 25, *25*
Alectrosaurus, 24-25
Alioramus, 24, 25
Allosaurus, 9, 22, *22*, 23, *23*, 29
Alocodon, 34, *35*
Ammosaurus, 26-27, *27*
Anatosaurus, 40, *40*, 41, *41*
Anchiceratops, 48, *48*, 49, *49*
Anchisaurus, *26*, 27
Ankylosaurids, 32, 35, 55, 58-59, *58, 59*
Ankylosaurs, 8, 9, 56-59
Ankylosaurus, 59
Antarctica, 10, 61
Antarctosaurus, *29*
Apatosaurus, 9, 28-29, *29*, 30
Argentina, 10, 32, 61
Aristosuchus, *13*
Arrhinoceratops, 48, *49*
Asia, 10, 24, 38, 40, 42, 44, 52
Atlantosaurus, *29*
Australia, 10, 12, 36, 56, 61
Avimimus, 16, *16*, 17, *17*

Bactrosaurus, 40, *40*, 41
Bagaceratops, *44*
Barapasaurus 32, *32*, 61
Barosaurus, *29*
Baryonyx, *21*, 23
Bernissart, Belgium, 39
Brachiosaurii, 30-31
Brachiosaurus, 10, *30*, 31, *31*
Brachylophosaurus, *41*
Brachyrhinoceratops, 46, 47, *47*
Britain, 6, 20, 32, 36, 52, 54, 57, 61
Brontosaurus, 29

Callovosaurus, 38, *39*
Camarasaurii, 30-31
Camarasaurus, 9, 29, 30, *30, 31*
Camptosaurus, *23, 38, 39*
Canada, 10, 18, 20, 47, 49, 50, 58, 61
Carnivores, see theropods
Carnosaurs, 20, 22-23, *22, 23*
Centrosaurus, 46, 47, *46, 47*
Ceratopids, 8, 44-49
    long frilled, 48-49
    protoceratopids, 43-44, 49
    short frilled, 46-47
Ceratosaurus, 22, 23, *23*
Cetiosauriscus, *29*, 32, *32*
Chasmosaurus, 48, *48*, 49, *49*
Chialingosaurus, *53*
China, 6, 10, 12, 14, 15, 16, 18, 20, 22, 34, 52, 61
Chirostenotes, *17*
Coelophysis, 12-13, *12, 13*, 17
Coelurosaurs, 12-13, *12-13*, 20
Coloradia, 27
Corythosaurus, 42, *42*, 43, *43*
Craspedodon, 38, *39*
Craterosaurus, *53*
Cretaceous Period, 8, 10-11
Cumnoria, *39*

Dacentrurus, *53*
Daspletosaurus, *24*, 25, *25*
Datousaurus, 32
Deinocheirus, *15*
Deinonychus, 19, 20-21, *20. 21, 36*
Diceratops, *47*

Dicraeosaurus, 29, *29*
Dilophosaurus, 22, *22*, 23
Dinosaur National Monument, Utah (USA), 9, 29, 30
Dinosauroid, 18, *18*
Dinosaurs
    classification of, 8, 16-17
    discovery of, 6, 8, 9-10, 61
    evolution and, 8, 10, 18, 26
    extinction and, 10, 11, 60
Diplodocids, 28-29, *28, 29*
Diplodocus, 9, 28 *29*
Drachopelta, 56
Dravidosaurus, *53*
Dromaeosaurus, 20-21, *20-21*
Dromaeosaurus, 20-21, *20, 21*
Dromiceiomimus, 14-15, *14, 15*
Dryosaurus, *26*, 37, *37*
Dynonychus, 19
Dysalotosaurus, 36, *37*

Earth
    geological processes on, 6
    history of, 10
Echinodon, 34, *35*
Edmontosaurus 40, 41, *40, 41*, 42
Elaphrosaurus, 13, 14, 15
Elmisaurus, *17*
Eoceratops, 48, *49*
Erlikosaurus, 16-17, *16, 17*
Euhelopus, 30
Euoplocephalus, 58-59, *58, 59*
Europe, 9, 10, 12, 22, 30, 34, 36, 38, 40, 44, 52, 54, 56, 61
Eustreptospondylus, *23*
Evolution, 6-7, 10-11, 18, 26
Extinction, 10, 11
    climatic change theory, 60
    cosmic theory, 60

Fabrosaurii, 34-35
Fossilisation, 6, *6*,
    geological time scales of, 6-7, 6, 10
Fossils, 6, 6, 8, 9, 10, 45
Fulgurotherium, 36, *37*

Gallimimus, 14
Garudimimus, 14
Gastroliths, 44
Genyodectes, 24-25
Geranosaurus, 34, *35*
Germany, 9, 26, 44, 61
Gobi Desert, 21, 25, 61
Gongbusaurus, 34, *35*
Goyocephale, *51*
Gravitholus, *5*
Gullimimus, 14, 15, *15*

Hadrosaurids, 40-43
    crested, 42-43, *42*
    flat-headed, 40-41
Hadrosaurus, *41*
Halsanpes, *21*
Halticosaurus, *13*
Haplocanthosaurus, *31*
Heterodontosaurii, 34-35
Heterodontosaurus, 8, *8, 34*, 35, *35, 37*
Hip structures, 8, *8*, 55
Homalocephale, 50, *50*, 51, *51*
Huayangosaurus, *53*
Hylaeosaurus, 6, 9, 56, *56*, 57
Hypsilophodon, 36-37, *36, 37*
Hypsilophodontids, 10, 36-37, 51

Ichthyosaurs, 54, 60

Iguanodon, 38, *38*, 39, *39*
Iguanodontii, 6, 9, *9*, 38-39, *38, 39*, 61
India, 10, 24, 32, 52, 61
Indosuchus, 24, *25*
Ioncosaurus, 36
Itemirus, 24-25

Jurassic Period, 10-11

Kakuru, *12*
Kangnasaurus, *39*
Kentrosaurus, 52, *52*, 53, *53*
Krittosaurus, 40, *40*, 41, *41*

Labocania, 24, *25*
Lambeosaurus, 42, 43, *43*
Laplatasaurus, 32, *32*
Leptoceratops, 44
Lesothaurus, 34-35, *34*
Lesothosaurus, 55
Lexovisaurus, *53*
Loncosaurus, 36, *37*
Lufengosaurus, 27
Lukousaurus, *13*
Lusitanosaurus, 54, 55

Macrophalangia, *17*
Madagascar, 51
Maiasaura, *43*
Majungatholus, 50, *51*
Malanorosaurus, 26-27, *27*
Mamenchisaurus, 29
Massospondylus, 27, *27*
Megalosaurus, 6, 9, *23*
Mesozoic era, 8
    continent positions, *10, 11*
Microceratops, 44
Micropachycephalosaurus, *51*
Minmi, 56
Mochlodon, *39*
Mongolia, 10, 15, 18, 24, 32, 41, 44, 45, 50, 51, 60
Monoclonius, 46, 47, *47*
Montanoceratops, 44
Mussaurus, 27, *27*
Muttaburrasaurus, 38, 39, *39*

Nanosaurus, 34, *35*
Nemegtosaurus, 29, *29*, 32
Nodosaurids, 55, 56-57, *56, 57*
Nodosaurus, 56, *56*, 57, *57*
North America, 9, 10, 14, 16, 17, 18, 20, 22, 24, 30, 31, 34, 36, 38, 40. 42, 44, 46, 48, 52, 54, 56, 57, 60. 61

Omeisaurus, 32, *32, 33*
Opisthocoelicaudia, 30, 32, 32, 33
Ornatholus, *51*
Ornithischians, 8, *8*
    ankylosaurs, 8, 35, 56-59
    ceratopians, 8, 44-49
    ornithopods, 8, 34-43
    pachycephalosaurs, 8, 50-51
    stegosaurs, 8, 52-53
Ornitholestes, 12-13, *12, 13*
Ornithomimosaurs, 14-15, *14*, 18
Ornithomimus, 15
Ornithopods, 8, 34-43, 61
Ornithopsis, 32 *32*
Orodromeus, 36
Othnelia, 36, *37*
Ouranosaurus, *38, 39, 39*
Oviraptorosaurs, 14-15, *14*

Pachycephalosaurs, 8, 50-51, *50, 51*

Pachyrhinosaurus, 46, 47, *47*
Pangaea, *10,* 11
Panoplosaurus, 56, *57*
Paranthodon, 53
Parasaurolophus, 42, *42*, 43
Parkosaurus, 36, *37*
Patagonia, 27
Pelorosaurus, 30
Pentaceratops, 48, *49, 49*
Permineralisation, 6
Petrification, 6, *6*
Phaedrolosaurus, *21*
Pinacosaurus, 10, 58
Plateosaurus, 26, 37, *26, 27*, 61
Plesiosaurs, 54, 60
Polacanthus, 56, *56*, 57, *57*
Prenocephale, 50, 51, *51*
Priveteausaurus, *23*
Probactrosaurus, 38, *39*
Proceratosaurus, *23*
Procheneosaurus, *43*
Procompsognathus, *13*
Prodeinodon, 24, *25*
Prosaurolophus, 42, 43, *43*
Prosauropods, 8, 17, 26-27, *26, 27*, 61
Protoceratopids, 10, 21, 44-45, *44, 45, 47*
Psittacosaurs, 44-45, *44, 45*
Psittacosaurus, 10, 44, *44, 45*
Pterosaurs, 8, 60

Rebbachisaurus, 30, *31*
Riojasuarus, 26-27, *27*

Saichania, 59
Saltasaurus, 32, *32, 33*
Saltopus, *11*
Sarcolestes, 56
Saurischians, 8, *8*, 12-25, 26-27, 28-33
Saurolophus, 42, 43, *42, 43*
Sauropelta, 56
Sauroplites, 59
Sauropodomorphs, 8
Sauropods, 8, 28-33
    miscellaneous, 32-33
Saurornithoidids, 18-19
Scelidosaurus, 54-55, *54, 55*
Scutellosaurus, 34-35, *34, 35*, 55
Secernosaurus, *41*
Sedimentation, 66
Segisaurus, 16-17, *16, 17*
Segnosaurus, 16-17
Shamosaurus, 59
Shantungosaurus, 40, *41*
Shunosaurus, 32
Silvisaurus, 56
South America, 16, 24, 36, 40, 61
Spinosaurus, *23*
Stegoceras, 50, *50*, 51, *51*
Stegosaurs, 8, 9, 52-53, *52, 53*
Stenonychosaurus, 18, *19*
Stenopelix, 44
Stromalites, 6, *6*
Struthiomimus, 14-15, *14, 15*
Struthiosaurus, 56
Stryracosaurus, 46, *46*, 47, *47*
Styginoloch, *51*
Supersaurus, 30, 31, *31*
Syntarus, 13
Szechuanosaurus, *23*

Talarurus, 59
Tanzania, 10, 31, 61
Tarbosaurus, 24, 25, *25*
Tarchia, 59

Tectonic plates, 10, 60
Tenontosaurus, *36*, 37, *37*
Therizinosaurus, *17*
Theropods, 8, 9, 12-25
    miscellaneous, 16-17, *16, 17*
    prosauropods, 8, 26-27
    sauropodomorphs, 8
    sauropods, 8, 28-33
Thescelosaurus, 36, *37*
Titanosaurus, *32*
Torosaurus, 48, *48*, 49, *49*
Triassic Period, 8, 10-11
Triceratops, 46, *46*, 47
Trimucrodon, 34, *35*
Trooden, 50, *51*
Tsintaosaurus, 42, *42*, 43
Tuojiangosaurus, 52, *52*, 53, *53*
Tylocephale, *51*
Tyrannosaurids, 24-25, *24, 25*, 47, 59
Tyrannosaurus, 24, *24*, 25

Ultrasaurus, 30, 31, *31*
Unquillosaurus, 24, *25*

Valdosaurus, 36, *37*
Vectisaurus, *39*
Velociraptors, 10, *20*, 21, *21*
Vulcanodon, 32, *32*

Wuerhosaurus, *53*
Wyoming, USA, 9, 24, 30, 46, 52, 57, 61

Xiaosaurus, 36, 37

Yangchuanosaurus, 23
Yavalandia, 50, *51*
Yunnanosaurus, 26-27, *27*

Zephyrosaurus, 36, *37*
Zigongosaurus, *31*

Picture Credits
British Museum (Natural History): 8
Stephen Hult, Museum of Isle of Wight Geology: 37
Imitor: 8
Los Angeles County Museum: 23
Mansell Collection: 9
Pat Morris Photographic: 31
Moscow Academy of Sciences: 44
Senckenberg Museum, Frankfurt: 39
Smithsonian Institution: 47
South African Museum: 27, 35
Tyrrell Museum of Palaeontology, Alberta: 25, 41, 43